# Beauty

# WILL SAVE THE
# WORLD

10/2020

# Beauty
# WILL SAVE THE
# WORLD

## BRIAN ZAHND

CHARISMA
HOUSE

Most CHARISMA HOUSE BOOK GROUP products are available at special quantity discounts for bulk purchase for sales promotions, premiums, fund-raising, and educational needs. For details, write Charisma House Book Group, 600 Rinehart Road, Lake Mary, Florida 32746, or telephone (407) 333-0600.

BEAUTY WILL SAVE THE WORLD by Brian Zahnd
Published by Charisma House
Charisma Media/Charisma House Book Group
600 Rinehart Road
Lake Mary, Florida 32746
www.charismahouse.com

Unless otherwise noted, all Scripture quotations are from the New Revised Standard Version of the Bible. Copyright © 1989 by the Division of Christian Education of the National Council of the Churches of Christ in the USA. Used by permission.

Scripture quotations marked ESV are from the Holy Bible, English Standard Version. Copyright © 2001 by Crossway Bibles, a division of Good News Publishers. Used by permission.

Scripture quotations marked KJV are from the King James Version of the Bible.

Scripture quotations marked NIV are from the Holy Bible, New International Version. Copyright © 1973, 1978, 1984, International Bible Society. Used by permission.

Scripture quotations marked NKJV are from the New King James Version of the Bible. Copyright © 1979, 1980, 1982 by Thomas Nelson, Inc., publishers. Used by permission.

Scripture quotations marked THE MESSAGE are from *The Message: The Bible in Contemporary English*, copyright © 1993, 1994, 1995, 1996, 2000, 2001, 2002. Used by permission of NavPress Publishing Group.

Cover design by Justin Evans

Visit the author's website at www.brianzahnd.com.

Library of Congress Cataloging-in-Publication Data:
Zahnd, Brian.
  Beauty will save the world / Brian Zahnd.
    p. cm.
  Includes bibliographical references (p.    ).
  ISBN 978-1-61638-585-9 (trade paper) -- ISBN 978-1-61638-641-2
(e-book) 1. Aesthetics--Religious aspects--Christianity. 2. Christianity-
-Essence, genius, nature. 3. Church and the world. I. Title.
  BR115.A8Z34 2012
  261.5'7—dc23
                                                      2011029697

While the author has made every effort to provide accurate Internet
addresses at the time of publication, neither the author nor the publisher
assumes any responsibility for errors or for changes that occur after
publication.

19 20 21 22 23 — 8 7 6 5 4
Printed in the United States of America

*For Brad Jersak and Joe Beach.*
*Thank you for your friendship and for helping me think.*

Out of Zion, the perfection of beauty, God shines forth.

—Psalm 50:2, esv

We do not want merely to see beauty, though, God knows, even that is bounty enough. We want something else which can hardly be put into words—to be united with the beauty we see, to pass into it, to receive it into ourselves, to bathe in it, to become part of it.[1]

—C. S. Lewis, *The Weight of Glory*

It is the prerogative and charm of beauty to win hearts.[2]

—Miguel de Cervantes, *Don Quixote*

# CONTENTS

A THOUSAND YEARS AGO Prince Vladimir the Great, the pagan monarch of Kiev, was looking for a new religion to unify the Russian people. Toward this end Prince Vladimir sent out envoys to investigate the great faiths from the neighboring realms. When the delegations returned, they gave the prince their reports. Some had discovered religions that were dour and austere. Others encountered faiths that were abstract and theoretical. But the envoys who had investigated Christianity in the Byzantine capital of Constantinople reported finding a faith characterized by such transcendent beauty that they did not know if they were in heaven or on earth.

> Then we went to Constantinople and they led us to the place where they worship their God, and we knew not whether we were in heaven or earth, for on earth there is no such vision nor beauty, and we do not know how to describe it; we only know that God dwells among men. We cannot forget that beauty.[1]

Upon receiving the report from the Constantinople delegation of the unearthly beauty they had witnessed in Christian worship, Prince Vladimir adopted Christianity as the new faith for the Russian people. What impressed the envoys and persuaded Prince Vladimir to embrace Christianity was not its apologetics or ethics, but its aesthetics—its beauty. Thus we might say it was beauty that brought salvation to the Russian people.

Nine hundred years later the great Russian writer Fyodor Dostoevsky coined the enigmatic expression, "beauty will save the world."[2] What Dostoevsky meant by this mysterious quip has been a matter of much conjecture, but it certainly must somehow have been connected to Dostoevsky's deep Christian faith.

Today there are many in the Western world who are searching for some form of spirituality to give them what materialism (the *de facto* religion of our age) promises but is unable to deliver. The gods of the Enlightenment have proved wanting, and like Prince Vladimir, many are in search of a new religion. The Western church as an heir of the Scientific Revolution remains tempted to respond to a renewed spiritual interest by supplying logical arguments for the truth of Christianity (apologetics) and perhaps by also making a case for the moral goodness of Christianity (ethics). This is all fine. But something is missing. What about beauty? Is it possible that what Prince Vladimir found most persuasive about Christianity in the tenth century and what Prince Myshkin hinted at in Dostoevsky's *The Idiot* is the very thing that could draw a new generation of spiritual seekers to faith in Jesus Christ? Is it possible that the Christian message can be communicated in terms of beauty? Along with apologetics and ethics, is there also an aesthetics that belongs to the gospel of Jesus Christ? The answer is an enthusiastic *yes!* Beauty is integral to the Christian message.

To a skeptical world we are generally more accustomed to defend Christianity in terms of its truth and goodness. But beauty also belongs to the Christian faith. And beauty has a way of sneaking past defenses and speaking in unique ways. To a generation suspicious of truth claims and unconvinced by moral assertions, beauty has a surprising allure. And everything about Jesus Christ is beautiful! His life, his miracles, his grace, his teaching—even his death and certainly his resurrection—are all inimitably beautiful. A Christianity that is deeply enchanted by Christ's beauty and thus formed and fashioned by this beauty has the opportunity to present to a skeptical and jaded world an aspect of the gospel that has been too rare for far too long. Where truth and goodness fail to win an audience, beauty may once again captivate and draw those it enchants into the kingdom of saving grace. It is possible to tell the Christian story in terms of aesthetics, because the story of Jesus Christ is breathtakingly beautiful!

On November 13, 2010, the eighty-voice Chorus of Niagara from Niagara Falls, Ontario, gave a performance of the "Hallelujah Chorus" from Handel's *Messiah*. This would not be particularly noteworthy except that it was done as a surprise performance in the food court of the Seaway Mall. The unsuspecting shoppers didn't see it coming. It was just another busy lunch hour in the food court at the mall. Then a young woman with a cell phone pressed to her ear stood up and began to sing hallelujah. While people were trying to figure out what is going on, the first singer is joined by a man who, moments earlier, had been eating his Arby's lunch. Then what appears to be a mall custodian joins the chorus. Eventually all eighty voices of the choir are performing a stunning rendition of Handel's masterpiece. The shoppers in the food court are stunned. They realize something special has happened. Some capture the performance on their cell phones. Others rise to join in the time-honored tradition of standing for the "Hallelujah Chorus." Some simply sit with faces full of wonder, while others wipe away tears. All are witnesses to a miracle—the modern banality of a shopping mall food court has been transformed into a cathedral of astonishing beauty.

A local photography company recorded the surprise performance in the Seaway Mall and posted it online. They hoped it might be viewed by as many as fifty thousand people. But within weeks it had been viewed tens of millions of times! Why the interest in this "stunt"? Perhaps the thing that makes the video somewhat amusing is also what makes it deeply moving—its odd incongruence. The juxtaposing of high art and a shopping mall, the surprise of sacred music in a food court, is an incongruence that seems to have a strange effect upon us. Why? Perhaps as modern people we harbor a deep-seated fear that we are losing all beauty. We have technology, convenience, security, and a measure of prosperity, but where is the beauty? Where is the beauty that we know we cannot really live without? With this latent fear lurking in our subconscious, a choir appearing out of nowhere and performing sacred Baroque music in a shopping mall is a beautiful surprise and not unlike the surprise performance the Gospel of Luke reports as occurring at the birth of Christ:

> And suddenly there was with the angel a multitude of the heavenly host praising God and saying, Glory to God in the highest, and on earth peace, good will toward men.
>
> —LUKE 2:13–14, KJV

This "random act of culture" in Ontario is a wonderful metaphor for how the church should position itself in the world. Instead of angry protesters shaking our fists at a secular culture, we should be joyful singers transforming the secular with the sacred. Instead of alienated separatists sequestered in Christian enclaves, we are to transform malls and food courts into cathedrals by our beautiful song. If the church of the twenty-first century will lay down its anger and frustration, and instead joyfully sing the melody of Christ in the malls of meaninglessness, we can perhaps once again astonish a weary world with the beauty of the gospel. Theologian Yves Congar advocates the idea of the church, not in protest or isolation to the world, but as the saving presence of Christ within the world.

> The Church is not a special little group, isolated, apart, remaining untouched amidst the changes of the world. The Church is the world as believing in Christ, or, what comes to the same thing, it is Christ dwelling in and saving the world by our faith.[3]

Beautiful! Our task is not to protest the world into a certain moral conformity, but to attract the world to the saving beauty of Christ. We do this best, not by protest or political action, but by enacting a beautiful presence within the world. The Western church has had a four-century experiment with viewing salvation in a scientific and mechanistic manner, presenting it as a plan, system, or formula. It would be much better if we would return to viewing salvation as a song we sing. The Book of Revelation (from which George Frideric Handel found the lyrics for his "Hallelujah Chorus") doesn't have any plans or formulas, but it has lots of songs. The task of the church is to creatively and faithfully sing the songs of the Lamb in the midst of a world founded upon the beastly principles of greed, decadence, and violence. What is needed is not an ugly protest, but a beautiful song; not a pragmatic system, but a transcendent symphony. Why? Because God is more like a musician than a manager, more like a composer of symphonies than a clerk keeping ledgers.

> God is more like a cantor who chants his Creation into existence and rejoices everlastingly over its beautiful harmony. His song continues, and its melody moves and inspires humankind to restore beauty and harmony to a Creation that is fallen and misshapen.[4]

Sin and Satan have stolen from humanity the song we were meant to sing with our Creator. We are bereft of beauty and missing melody. We are left with little more than the inane Muzak of the malls of meaninglessness. Friedrich Nietzsche is right when he says, "Without music life would be a mistake."[5] It is into this world that the Son of God comes singing his song—a song that first announces itself as beautiful. The Singer invites us to join him in his song. It is an invitation to find salvation—for to join the Son of God in singing his beautiful song is to find the melody that can save our soul. This is the beauty that saves the world.

> After the seas are all cross'd, (as they seem already
> cross'd,)
> After the great captains and engineers have
> accomplish'd their work,
> After the noble inventors, after the scientists, the
> chemists, the geologist, ethnologist,
> Finally shall come the poet worthy of that name,
> The true son of God shall come singing his songs.[6]
>
> —WALT WHITMAN

## CHAPTER 1

# FORM AND BEAUTY

THIS IS A book about beauty and Christianity—or perhaps about the beauty *of* Christianity. We are all attracted to beauty. We desire it, we admire it, we recognize it when we see it. We have an innate instinct for beauty, even if the definition of what beauty actually is can be a bit unwieldy. In an academic sense, beauty is generally understood as a combination of color, shape, and form that we find aesthetically pleasing. That is a rather bland description of beauty, but even if the definition is inadequate, we do understand that beauty has a form. This is important. Whether it's a painting or a poem or a sculpture or a song, beauty has a form. Form is central to beauty. Distortion of a beautiful form takes away from its beauty. Obviously it's even possible for a beautiful thing to become so distorted and deformed that it loses most or all of its beauty. When this happens, it's a kind of vandalism.

Think of a beautiful stained-glass window, an artistic combination of color, shape, and form. Imagine a stained-glass masterpiece in a great cathedral, perhaps depicting a scene from the life of Jesus. Now try to imagine a vandal lobbing bricks through that window. The beautiful combination of color and form has been broken, and beauty has been lost. It is a tragedy, and we are saddened. What we hope for now is some kind of restoration—we hope that beauty can be recovered. We hope for this because one way of viewing life is as an ongoing struggle to create, preserve, and recover what is beautiful. This is why art is not merely a leisure pursuit but serious business, because, quite simply, life should be made as beautiful as possible.

But this is not a book about art appreciation. This is a book about Christianity and about making it beautiful. Christianity in its proper form is a transcendent beauty. The story of Jesus's life, death, and resurrection is not only the greatest story ever told, but it's also the most beautiful story ever told. *Christianity as the ongoing expression of the Jesus story lived out in the lives of individuals and in the heart of society is a beauty that can redeem the world.* That is an almost outlandish statement, but I believe it!

Yet I also recognize that Christianity can be distorted. It can be twisted out of shape. It can lose its beautiful form. When this happens, Christianity is not only less than beautiful; it can at times be blatantly ugly. It has happened before. What I fear is that we are in danger of losing our perspective of what is most beautiful about Christianity and accidentally vandalizing our faith with the best of intentions. I fear the vandalism has already begun. This book is about what can be done and how Christianity can recover its form and beauty through a new kind of reformation.

*Ecclesia reformata semper reformanda*—The church reformed and always reforming.

This Latin phrase was one of the mottoes of the Protestant Reformation—a reminder and an acknowledgment that for the church to remain true to its mission and witness and to retain its beauty, the church must constantly be reforming itself. Of course, *semper reformanda* doesn't mean the church should mindlessly engage in change for the sake of faddish novelty or trendy innovation. That's not what I'm talking about. Rather *semper reformanda* comes from the realization that there are forces—political, social, theological, spiritual, and so forth—that over time tend to twist the church and the gospel out of shape. As a result the church must continually seek to recover the true form and original beauty found in the gospel of Jesus Christ. This kind of reformation is an ongoing process.

There is indeed a sense in which the need for some measure of reformation is always present, but there are also times when the need for reformation (think *re-formation*) is more critical than others. There are times when the distortion of the church is severe enough that the integrity of our message is compromised. I'm convinced the evangelical church in the Western world is facing just such a crisis. Putting it as plainly as I can, evangelical Christianity needs to recover the form and beauty that are intrinsic to Christianity. We need a reformation because we are being twisted out of shape. Let me try to explain how this has happened.

The stories of evangelicalism and America are deeply intertwined in much the same way that the stories of Catholicism and the Roman Empire are intertwined. Evangelical Christianity came of age during America's rise to superpower status on the world stage. America, untethered from European Christendom and their vassal state churches, provided an environment conducive for evangelical Christianity, and evangelical Christianity has flourished in the American environment. (By evangelical I mean the expression of Protestant Christianity characterized by a dual emphasis on the authority of Scripture and a personal conversion experience—this is evangelicalism at its best.) So far so good. But there is always a particular temptation faced by the church when it is hosted by a superpower. The temptation is to accommodate itself to its host and to adopt (or even christen) the cultural assumptions of the superpower.

This is nothing new. The long history of the church bears witness to the reality and seductive power of this temptation. The historic problem the Greek Orthodox Church struggled with in the East sixteen hundred years ago was the temptation to be too conformed to the Byzantine Empire. At the same time, the historic problem the Roman Catholic Church struggled with in the West was the temptation to be too conformed to the Roman Empire. And I dare to suggest (or even insist!) that the problem that is distorting American evangelicalism is that it has become far too accommodating to Americanism and the culture of a superpower. This is fairly obvious. You don't have to be a sociologist to recognize that the American obsession with pragmatism, individualism, consumerism, materialism, and militarism that so characterizes contemporary America has come to shape (and thereby distort) the dominant form of evangelical Christianity found in North America. It becomes American culture with a Jesus fish bumper sticker. If we are unwilling to engage in critical thought, we will simply assume that this *is* Christianity, when in reality it is a *kind* of Christianity blended with many other things.

To be born in America is to be handed a certain script. We are largely unconscious of the script, but we are "scripted" by it nevertheless. The American script is part of our nurture and education, and most of it happens without our knowing it. The dominant American script is that which idolizes success, achievement, acquisition, technology, and militarism. It is the script of a superpower. But this dominant script does not fit neatly with the alternative script we find in the gospel of Jesus Christ. So here is our challenge: when those who confess Christ find themselves living in the midst of an economic and military superpower, they are faced with the choice to either be an accommodating chaplain or a prophetic challenge. Over the last generation or so, evangelicalism has been more adept at endorsing the dominant script than challenging it. And in conforming too closely to the dominant script of Americanism, the Christianity of the American church has become disfigured and distorted and is in desperate need of recovering its true form and original beauty through a process of re-formation. We need to bear the form and beauty of the Jesus way and not merely provide a Christianized version of our cultural assumptions.

In order to recover the true form and original beauty that is integral to Christianity, we need an ideal form, a true standard, an accurate template, a faithful model to which we can look, to which we must conform. For historic Christianity this has always been Jesus Christ upon the cross, which is a holy irony, since crucifixion was designed to be ghastly and hideous. But this is the mystery of the cross. The crucifixion of Jesus Christ, which attains in retrospect an eternal glory and beauty through the resurrection, is the axis of Christianity around which everything else revolves. Thus the cruciform (the shape of a cross) is the eternal form that endows Christianity with its mysterious beauty. Simply put, the cross is the form that makes Christianity beautiful! The cross is the beauty of Christianity because it is at the cross that we encounter co-suffering love and costly forgiveness in its most beautiful form.

But the question is, can we see the beauty of the cruciform? In a culture that idolizes success, can we see beauty in the cross? In a culture that equates beauty with a "pretty face," can we see past the horror of a grisly execution and discern the sacred beauty beneath the surface? This is what artistic representations of the cruciform are capable of capturing and why their work is invaluable. The artist doesn't give us a journalistic photograph of an event, but an artistic interpretation of an event. The great masters of sacred art were both artists and theologians; through their work they have given us an artistic interpretation that reveals the inherent, but hidden, beauty of the cross. Consider the cruciform and try to apprehend its beauty. The Christ upon the cross, arms outstretched in the gesture of proffered embrace, refusing to call upon avenging angels but instead loving his enemies and praying for their forgiveness—this is the form and beauty of Christianity. The cruciform is the posture of love and forgiveness where retaliation is abandoned and outcomes are entrusted to the hands of God. The cross is laden with mystery. At first glance it looks like anything but success. It looks like failure. It looks like defeat. It looks like death. It *is* death. But it is also the power and wisdom of God.* This is mysterious. It is also beautiful. This is the mysterious beauty that saves the world.

---

* 1 Corinthians 1:24

The cruciform is the aesthetic of our gospel. It is the form that gives Christianity its unique beauty. It is what distinguishes Christianity from the dominant script of a superpower. But the beauty of the cruciform is a beauty communicated in a mystery. To those who value only conventional power and crass pragmatism—which is always the tendency of a superpower—the cruciform looks like folly, weakness, defeat, and death. It is not conventional beauty. But to those who have eyes to see, the cruciform shows forth a transcendent beauty—the beauty of love and forgiveness. It is the beauty of Christ's love and forgiveness as most clearly seen in the cruciform that is able to save us from our vicious pride and avaricious greed.

This is relevant to our situation because pride and greed are often pawned off as virtues in the culture of a superpower. Pride and greed are the engines of expansion, and as such they tend to be reworked as attributes. It was true in first-century Rome, and it's true in twenty-first-century America. We're told to "take pride in ourselves" and reminded that "we're number one." We sing about how proud we are to be Americans (even in church!). Plus there's always someone new buying into Ayn Rand's objectivist philosophy of self-interest and explaining to us with great passion how "greed is good." But our Scriptures give a minority report; they tell us that pride and greed are the pliers that have distorted our humanity into a sinful ugliness. We must see the beauty of Christ in the cruciform and understand that it is only the beauty of self-sacrificing love that can save us from pride and greed. This is the beauty Dostoevsky correctly and prophetically spoke of when he said, "Beauty will save the world."

The church always faces the temptation to turn its gaze from the beauty of the cruciform and look instead to "the kingdoms

of the world and their splendor."* The beauty of the cruciform is a subtle and hidden beauty, like the enigmatic smile of
Mona Lisa. The splendor of Babylon is brash, like the garish
lights of Las Vegas. When we lose sight of the subtle beauty
of the cruciform we become seduced by the power, prestige,
and pragmatism of politics. To borrow Tolkien's theme, we
become seduced by the ring of power. The ring of power is the
enemy of beauty. It was the ring of power—"my precious"—
that transformed the humanlike Sméagol into the reptilian
Gollum. In like manner, the church begins to devolve from
beauty into a distorted form less beautiful the moment it
reaches for the ring of power. *Lord of the Rings*

But we reach for the ring of power nevertheless. We find it
almost irresistible. Of course we supply ourselves with copious
reasons as to why our fascination with conventional power
is a good thing: "We want to have power to do good." "We
want to make a difference in the world." "We have to take
a stand against evil." But without realizing it, we are being
subtly seduced into thinking there is a better way to go about
achieving righteousness and justice (think beauty) than by
taking up the cross and following Jesus. We begin to think
that if we can just get Caesar on our side, if we can just get
the emperor to hold a National Prayer Breakfast, we can then
baptize the ways and means of the empire and at last accomplish "great things for God." And here's the thing: Caesar is
more than willing to employ the church as a chaplain, as long
as the church will endorse (with a bit of religious flourish) the
ways and means of the empire. Of course the ways and means
of the empire are the ways and means of political and military

---

* Matthew 4:8

domination. There's no beauty in that. Politics is never pretty. Everyone knows that. Thus the church sacrifices the beauty of Christianity when it chooses the political form over the cruciform. Reaching for the ring of power distorts our beauty.

But why would we do it? Why would we sacrifice the enchanting beauty of Christianity for the ugly machine of politics? Because political power is so—and there's no other word for it—*pragmatic*. We're convinced "it works." What could be more simple? Here's the formula. Just put good people in positions of power and good things will happen. (Such thinking is very close to the wilderness temptation Jesus faced; more on that later.) We are easily seduced by the clear logic of political pragmatism. But we need to remember that God does not save the world through the clear logic of political pragmatism (though Jesus was tempted by the devil, and even by his own disciples, to attempt it). Instead, God saves the world through the ironic and mysterious beauty of the cruciform. To achieve good through attaining political and military dominance has always—*always!*—been the way of the fallen world. We seem to lack the imagination to envisage any other way. But it's not the Jesus way. It's not the beautiful way. It's not the way of the cruciform.

Jesus does *not* save the world by adopting the ways and means of political pragmatism and becoming the best Caesar the world has ever seen. Instead Jesus saves the world by suffering the worst crime humanity is capable of—the crime of deicide (the murder of God). On the cross Jesus absorbed our hate and hostility, our vengeance and violence into His own body and recycled it into love and forgiveness. By his wounds we are healed.* By this beauty we are saved.

The third-century theologian Origen observed that "the marvel of Christ is that, in a world where power, riches, and violence seduce hearts and compel assent, he persuades and prevails not as a tyrant, an armed assailant, or a man of wealth, but simply as a teacher of God and his love."[1] Commenting on this, David Bentley Hart says, "Christ is a persuasion, a form evoking desire.... Such an account [of Christ] must inevitably make an appeal to beauty."[2] I absolutely agree! Christ persuades, not by the force of Caesar, but by the beauty of love.

I assume that every Christian would agree with the idea that what Jesus did in his death was beautiful and that somehow this beautiful act is central to our salvation. But the challenge is to translate the beauty of the cruciform into contemporary Christianity—especially a contemporary Christianity obsessed with power and politics. The beauty of the cruciform by which Jesus saves the world through an act of co-suffering love and costly forgiveness is the same beauty that must characterize the church if we are to show forth the glory of the Lord in our world. But it's the beauty of cruciform love that is most marred when we allow the Christian faith to be politicized.

A politicized faith loses its beauty very quickly. I know, because I was once an enthusiastic participant in the process of faith-based politicization. I was willing to subtly, and at times not so subtly, align my church with partisan political agendas. Senators and congressman would visit my church to give their testimonies (always around election time). We handed out "voter guides" so those not paying close enough

---

* 1 Peter 2:24

attention would know how to vote. We found ways to make the elephants and donkeys of the American political process somehow analogous to the sheep and goats in Jesus's parables. But for me that came to an abrupt end in a fairly dramatic fashion.

In September of 2004 *Cheney* in the heat of a volatile presidential campaign I was asked to give the invocation at a political rally where one of the vice presidential candidates was appearing. I agreed to do so. I remember well the acrimony outside the convention center where protestors and supporters were busy hurling ugly epithets at one another. Inside the convention center the crowd was being whipped into a political frenzy that amounted to "hurray for our side!" As I sat on the platform with the political acolytes, and me as their rent-a-chaplain, I began to squirm. I knew I was being used. I was a pawn in a political game. I felt like a tool. (And a fool!)

When it came time for me to pray (for which the unstated purpose was to let it be known that God was squarely on our side), I stepped to the podium and first prayed silently, "God, what am I doing here? I've made a mistake. I'm sorry." I then offered a largely innocuous prayer and left as soon as I could, promising myself and God that I would never do anything like that again. But in leaving the convention center I again had to run the gauntlet of supporters and protesters yelling at one another with the police in between the two groups to prevent them from being at one another's throats. It wasn't pretty. And no prayer could make it pretty. It was petty, partisan, and petulant. I could not imagine Jesus or the apostles sullying their gospel to participate in it.

That moment was a turning point for me. I was no longer willing to see the church as a sidekick to Caesar, fully baptized (immersed, not sprinkled) into the acrimonious world of partisan politics. It's not that I'm afraid of controversy or persecution—I am perfectly willing to suffer persecution and ridicule for the sake of Christ (this is part of the cruciform). But I am unwilling to throw myself into the political fray for the sake of partisanship. I'm unwilling to do so because I simply no longer believe that political parties have much to do with God's redemptive work in the world. Jesus is building his church, not a political party. And I'm absolutely certain that political partisanship costs us our prophetic voice. We end up a tool to one side, an enemy to the other, and prophetic to neither. The bottom line is there is simply no way to make politics beautiful. But the way of the cruciform *is* beautiful. And I have made my choice. I choose the beautiful over the pragmatic. I realize that many people will not understand this, but I fully believe this is precisely the choice Jesus made. In choosing the cruciform over the political, Jesus was choosing the beautiful over the pragmatic.

If we are going to recover the form and beauty of Christianity, we are going to have to face squarely the issue of the politicization of the faith, because things are getting ugly. In the current climate of polarized partisanship where everything is now politicized, there is an appalling amount of anger, vitriol, and a general lack of civility. Sadly, millions of confessed followers of Jesus are being swept up in the madness as they give vent to their anger, fully convinced that God is on their side. Their justification is "we've got to take America back for God." Presumably this is to be done by the dubious means of acrimonious partisan politics. But we need to think less politically and more biblically.

Does the church have a mandate to change the world

through political means? We have assumed so, but it is a questionable assumption at best. Baptist theologian Russell Moore has observed that, "Too often, and for too long, American 'Christianity' has been a political agenda in search of a gospel useful enough to accommodate it."[3] But is our mission a kind of political agenda or is it something else? Isn't our first task to actually *be* God's alternative society? Pause and think about that. I'm afraid we've made a grave mistake concerning our mission. We're not so much tasked with running the world as with being a faithful expression of the kingdom of God through following Jesus and living the beautiful life that Jesus sets forth in the Sermon on the Mount. Jesus described his disciples as sheep among wolves.* The mistake of confusing our mission of being faithful as God's alternative society with trying to rule the world through the crude means of political power is nothing new—it's the mistake the church has been making for seventeen centuries. Prior to the Roman emperor Constantine, the early church was content to simply be the church—to be a city set upon a hill living the alternative lifestyle that is the Jesus way. But after the emperor Constantine and the adoption of Christianity as the imperial religion, the church embarked upon a project of running the world in cahoots with Caesar. This project has not turned out well. And it has been particularly damaging to the church. In fact, it has led to the ugliest episodes in church history. The church's collusion with political agendas led us into the shameful venture of the Crusades and the arrogant doctrine of Manifest Destiny. These things are truly ugly.

The problem with our "change the world" rhetoric is that

---

\* Matthew 10:16

it is too often a thinly veiled grasp for power and a quest for dominance—things that are antithetical to the way Jesus calls his disciples to live. A politicized faith feeds on a narrative of perceived injury and lost entitlement leading us to blame, vilify, and seek to in some way retaliate against those we imagine responsible for the loss in late modernity of a mythical past. It's what Friedrich Nietzsche as a critic of Christianity identified as *ressentiment*, and it drives much of the Christian quest for political power. In the Jesus way the end—no matter how noble—*never* justifies the means. It's inevitable that a movement fueled by resentment will soon depart from the Jesus way, and it is bound to become ugly. Jesus specifically told us that we are not to emulate the ugly ways of Caesar in grasping for power and dominance. Instead we are to choose the counterintuitive way of humility, service, and sacrificial love. These things are inherently beautiful. But we have a hard time learning this lesson.

When the disciples James and John (whom for obvious reasons Jesus called "the sons of thunder") expressed a desire to reign with Christ in their imagined version of Jesus as Caesar, Jesus made it clear that they didn't know what they were talking about and that the way of political dominance would *not* be the way of his kingdom.* Jesus curtly told his disciples: "It shall not be so among you."† Jesus was doing something new and truly beautiful; he was not imitating the way and means of Caesar. The brutal Roman Empire had plenty of splendor as veneer, but it lacked any true depth of beauty. Jesus deliberately chose the beauty of co-suffering love over the brutal pragmatism of political power. When Pilate encountered

---

* See Mark 10:35–45.
† Mark 10:43, NKJV

Christ, he could not understand this—but we must. We must never forget that Jesus ushered in his kingdom by refusing to oppose Caesar on Caesar's terms. Jesus didn't fight political power with political power. Thus Jesus submitted to the injustice of a state-sponsored execution by telling Pilate, "My kingdom is not from this world. If my kingdom were from this world, my followers would be fighting."* Think about that. It is part of the mystery and beauty of Christianity that the kingdom of God comes, not by the sword of political power, but by the cross of self-sacrificing love. Jesus didn't smash his foes with the sword of "righteous" political power; instead he absorbed the blow of injustice and committed his fate to the hands of God. In this we find an undeniable truth: *we cannot fight for the kingdom of Christ in the same manner that the nations of the world fight, for the moment we do, we are no longer the kingdom of Christ but the kingdom of the world!* A politicized mind can only imagine power as political domination, but a Spirit-renewed mind imagines the more excellent way of love—which is the more beautiful way of the cruciform.

Admittedly we live in a world where much is wrong. But what is most wrong with the world is not our politics or Congress or who lives in the White House. This is either the naïve gullibility or the manipulative rhetoric of partisanship. What is most wrong with the world is the ugly distortion of humanity brought about through the dehumanizing forces of lust, greed, and pride. As followers of Jesus we are not called to campaign for a political solution—for ultimately there is none—but to demonstrate an authentic Christian alternative. We are advocates of another way. Certainly we can participate

---

* John 18:36

in the political process, but we must do so primarily as ambassadors of another kingdom exhibiting and teaching the beautiful virtues of that kingdom. This is how we are salt and light. This is what makes us a shining city set upon a hill. We are to model what it means to be Christlike in a Caesar-like world. But to be Christlike in a Caesar-like world requires us to embrace the cruciform.

Of course the cruciform is offensive to the unimaginative mind of pragmatism. Pragmatism sees the cruciform as a passive surrender (though it is anything but that!). Pragmatism believes the only way to change the world is to beat down the bad guys—either with ballots or bullets. But without even raising the thorny issue of who are the bad guys in the ever-escalating world of revenge, the philosophy of "beat down the bad guys" displays an appalling lack of imagination. Pragmatism requires little imagination; it only needs the will to power. Or pragmatism will trot out the oft-quoted axiom from Edmund Burke: "All that is necessary for the triumph of evil is for good men to do nothing." That is true enough, provided we don't misapply what it means to "do nothing." I was once given Burke's maxim as a counterargument after preaching on the Sermon on the Mount. As if living the Sermon on the Mount is "doing nothing." Or worse yet, as if a Christian can call upon Edmund Burke to refute Jesus Christ!

But here is the real problem I have with the trajectory of the American evangelical church in the early twenty-first century. If, instead of imitating Christ with his cross, we want to imitate Caesar with his sword, we inevitably choose the ugly over the beautiful. This approach always leads the church away from living as a witness to the gospel. Being a faithful witness to the gospel should be a hallmark of evangelical Christianity.

But something has gone very wrong. Think about it—that the primary public witness of the American evangelical church for the past thirty years has been political is an absolute tragedy! Evangelicals are no longer known within the wider culture for their devotion to Scripture and their belief in a personal conversion experience. Now evangelicals are known primarily for their politics. This has been anything but helpful. The amount of hope many evangelical Christians place in politics is nothing short of astonishing! If nothing else, it is naïve—but worse, it is a betrayal. It is a betrayal of the beautiful way of Christ. For in a politicized faith we embrace the ugly pragmatism of political domination over the beauty of the cruciform.

Theologian Stanley Hauerwas has correctly observed: "The church doesn't have a social strategy; the church *is* a social strategy."[4] Instead of trying to force change upon the wider society through means of legislation, we are to exemplify the beautiful alternative of the kingdom of God *by actually living it!* We make a terrible mistake when we tell the wider society something like this: "We have the truth, so let us run society by setting the rules." That is a kind of tyranny, no matter how well intended. Instead we should simply *be* the alternative we seek to produce. We should *be* a righteous and just society. We should *be* the beautiful expression of the kingdom of God attracting people by the unique aesthetic of our gospel. Our form is the cruciform, and our beauty is the mysterious aesthetic of the crucified Savior.

Admittedly, this is a complicated issue that doesn't yield itself to simplistic solutions. I understand this. Christians have a complicated relationship with the state because we are a people who carry dual citizenship. We are citizens of both the kingdom of Christ and the particular geopolitical nation we happen to live in. But this much is certain: our first allegiance must be to the kingdom of Christ. Furthermore, we must never make the mistake of thinking God has some kind of commitment to the well-being of our particular nation over the well-being of other nations. This type of ugly and arrogant nationalism is completely incompatible with the Christian faith, which confesses Jesus as Savior of the world and not merely some version of a national deity. Is it possible that American Christians actually believe that Jesus has an interest in the well-being of America over the well-being of, say, Mexico or China or Ethiopia? Surely not! This is "American Exceptionalism" as a ridiculous and idolatrous doctrine. Our politicians may traffic in such nonsense, but Christians must not! What Jesus is committed to is the salvation of the world and the building up of his global church. So whereas Christians are free to participate in the civic and political process of their respective nations, Christians must do so as those who exhibit a primary allegiance to the Jesus way—the beautiful way of the cruciform. This means treating everyone (including political enemies) with kindness, love, and respect. As followers of Christ, our mission is not to seek to rule the world through Caesar's means of dominance—a means Jesus explicitly rejected—but to be a faithful church and thus a living example of God's alternative society.

So, reformation is needed, and the cruciform is what can give shape to our much-needed reformation. In the cruciform we find both our proper form and, subsequently, our unique beauty. The cruciform as a pattern gives us a means of evaluating our own form and how we present ourselves to the wider culture. With an eye on the cruciform, we can ask ourselves, "Does this attitude, this approach, this action look like Jesus on the cross?" If our attitude, approach, and action cannot be reasonably compared to the image of the cruciform, we need to abandon it. Caesar may adopt it, it may be practical, it may even be "successful," but if it's not Christlike, then it's not our pattern. Without a radical commitment to the shape of the cruciform, the process of deformation will continue year after year, and our beauty will be lost.

One of the "pliers" that distorts our Christian witness out of shape is the paradigm of protest. For far too long we have been enamored (and distorted) by protest. We love to protest. We really do. We're good at it. We have lots of practice at it. In protest we find an outlet for our anger, we connect with like-minded people, and we at least feel like we are "making a difference" and "standing up for righteousness." It's exciting and cathartic. So we picket, we protest, we boycott, we form petition drives, and we write angry letters to editors and CEOs and encourage other Christians to do the same. We hold rallies where we in no uncertain terms, and with presumed divine sanction, unleash our righteous anger on a wide range of enemies. Liberals, Hollywood, gays, and Muslims are regular targets. But does it look like the cruciform? Is it beautiful? Would a common observer look at it and say, "That's beautiful; it reminds me of Jesus"? Do our clenched fists and furrowed brows of protest align nicely with the outstretched arms and compassionate face of Christ on the cross? If not, we have drifted from the pattern of the cruciform in our paradigm of protest, and the inevitable result will be a distortion of Christianity. As our Christianity takes on more of a political agenda, it sloughs off resemblance to the cruciform. The result is a distinctive loss of beauty. We tend to justify our foray into the unseemly as necessary if we are to preserve morality, but I agree with Orthodox Archbishop Lazar Puhalo when he says, "True morality consists in how well we care for one another, not what sort of behaviour we wish to impose on one another."[5]

Again I raise the question: Why would we do this? Why would we sacrifice the beauty of the cruciform for something everyone knows is a far cry from beautiful? Why this obsession with political power? I think the answer is that we have a carnal obsession with outcomes. It's the ugly specter of pragmatism. We want to see a clear and obvious way that our actions are going to result in the desired outcome. We want to do good, achieve good, bring about good, vote in good, legislate good, formulate good, enforce good. So we choose the means that appear most logical in achieving this outcome. But remember, Satan never tempted Jesus with evil; Satan tempted Jesus with good. Satan enticed Jesus to go ahead and do good and to bring it about by the most direct way possible. The temptation was to imitate the means and methods of the pharaohs and Caesars. Satan tempted Jesus to usher in a righteous world by a bloody sword. "War is impatience."[6] Obsession with outcomes and demanding to see a quick and logical way in which present action will bring about desired good are the ways of Caesar, but they are not the way of the cruciform. Obsession with outcomes is, among other things, an abandonment of faith.

Christians all believe that Jesus achieved salvation through what he did on the cross. (Though the exact way this works remains a matter of theological debate.) But on Good Friday, how could anyone have seen a "logic" in Jesus's crucifixion? If Jesus's intent was to save the world from the dominion of evil, how could submitting to an unjust execution at the hands of an oppressive regime accomplish anything like that? It's absurd! Salvation is ironic because there is nothing logical or practical or obvious about the cross. Fighting is practical. Fighting is logical. Fighting has a long history of (at least temporarily) achieving desired ends. Peter was ready to fight, and presumably so were many others who followed Jesus from Galilee. But Jesus told Peter to put up his sword. There would be no bloody revolution. No violent resistance. Not even an angry protest. Instead Jesus went to the cross, forgave his enemies, and simply died. In rejecting the way of Caesar, "Christ showed that the world was a text that could be read differently: according to the grammar not of power, but agape."[7]

Did evil triumph because this good man did nothing? It certainly seemed so. But don't forget the dying prayer of Jesus: "Father, into your hands I commit my spirit!"[*] I think we can understand Jesus's prayer as something like this: "Father, I have obeyed you, I have shown the world your ways, but the world has rejected me and your ways. I forgive them, but I am dying. So now I entrust everything to you." This is the way of the cruciform. It is the way of faith.

In going to the cross, Jesus was not being practical; he was being faithful. Jesus didn't take a pragmatic approach to the problem of evil; Jesus took an aesthetic approach to the problem of evil. Jesus chose to absorb the ugliness of evil and turn it into something beautiful—the beauty of forgiveness. Jesus bore the sin of the world by it being *sinned into* him with wounds. Jesus bore the sin of the world without a word of recrimination, but only a prayer of forgiveness. He bore the sin of the world all the way down to death. So that the apostle

---

[*] Luke 23:46, ESV

Peter says, "By his wounds you have been healed."* This is the beauty of the cruciform. This is beauty being derived from pain, or as Bob Dylan says, "Behind every beautiful thing there's been some kind of pain."[8]

In order to do a beautiful thing, Jesus had to abandon outcomes. He had to entrust the outcome to his Father. On Good Friday Jesus abandoned outcomes, embraced the cross, and died. Jesus abandoned outcomes in order to be faithful and trust his Father. As we confess in the Apostles' Creed, "He was crucified, died, and was buried. He descended to the dead." A lost cause. But then came Easter! The cornerstone of Christian faith is that on Easter Sunday God vindicated his Son by raising him from the dead. But until Easter Sunday no one thought of death, burial, and resurrection as a logical means of achieving good. Even today most people cannot accept the "formula" of the cruciform as a viable means of bringing about good. We want something that makes more sense. Something quicker. Something practical. And what we get are the same old ugly ways of Pharaoh and Caesar. Our embrace of the practical and ugly over the faithful and beautiful exposes our unbelief. We are orthodox enough to confess that Jesus saves the world through his cross, but we don't want to imitate it. So we choose the ugly forms of coercion over the beauty of the cruciform—the false morality of the Pharisee over the true morality of Christ. But our critics see this ugliness in us, even if we are unaware of it.

Part of the problem is that in the Western world we are deeply conditioned to choose the heroic over the saintly. We love our heroes best of all. Heroes are goal-oriented people of

---

* 1 Peter 2:24

great capabilities who know how to make things happen. We admire their ability to get things done and shape the world according to their will. Saints on the other hand—especially to the American mind—seem quaint and marginal, occupying religious spheres on the periphery of the action. We want to be heroes; we don't really want to be saints. The difference between the heroic vision and the saintly vision is a fundamentally different way of viewing the purpose of life.

> For the hero, the meaning of life is honor...for the saint, the meaning of life is love.... For the hero, the goal of living is self-fulfillment, the achievement of personal excellence, and the recognition and admiration that making a signal contribution to one's society through one's achievements carries with it. For the saint, life does not so much have a goal as a purpose for which each human being is responsible; and that purpose is love: the bonds of concern and care that responsibility for one's fellow human beings carry with it.... These two paradigms—the hero and the saint—and the way of life that descends from each, are really two fundamentally distinct and genuinely different visions of human society as a whole, and even of what it means to be a human being. They are two distinct and different ways of asking the question of the meaning of life.[9]

Accepting Francis Ambrosio's paradigms for the hero and saint, we should recognize that the way of Jesus is the way of the saint, but the way of the hero is what we tend to glorify. To speak of the goal of life in terms of self-fulfillment, achievement, and excellence is very American (originally Greek and Roman) and very popular. There are plenty of versions of American Christianity that easily accommodate this basic paradigm. Christianity understood as a program for self-improvement and success in life is how Americanized Christianity most often accommodates itself to contemporary culture. It also makes Christianity popular and "successful." But an honest reading of the Sermon on the Mount makes it clear that Jesus is teaching something radically different. In the Gospels we see Jesus through his teaching, which sets forth the alternative paradigm of the saint where the purpose of life is love, and the expression of that love is in the form of care and compassion for our neighbor. The life of Jesus as recorded in the Gospels begins as a life of teaching and ends in a life of suffering. But these are not to be separated. At the cross Jesus lived all that he taught. The life of love that Jesus proclaimed in his teaching he lived in his suffering. The life of co-suffering love is the paradigm of the saint, and it is how Jesus lived and died. It is the beauty of the cruciform.

Of course I can hear someone protesting, "But Jesus is my *hero*!" I understand what is meant by that, but if we are intent upon forcing Jesus into the archetype of typical hero, we distort him. In trying to make Jesus a hero, we miss the simple fact that Jesus did nothing that was conventionally heroic—at least not according to the Western ideal of heroism. Elijah was a conventional hero when he humiliated the prophets of Baal on Mount Carmel and then executed them at the brook Kishon. But how did Jesus contend with his enemies at Calvary? Not in the heroic manner of Elijah on Carmel, but in a new and saintly way—the way of love and forgiveness. The Jesus of the Gospels is not a heroic general who slaughters his enemies, but a suffering saint who forgives his enemies. And even if one appeals to the Book of Revelation, it should be remembered that the holy irony perceived in the prophetic metaphors is that the monstrous beasts are conquered by a little slaughtered lamb. It should be clear that the way of Christ is not the way of the conventional hero, because Jesus saves the world not by shedding the blood of his enemies, but by allowing his own blood to be shed in an act of redemptive love. This is the way of the saint, not the hero.

But we struggle with choosing the way of the saint over the way of the hero. Our Christian rhetoric is replete with calls to the heroic as we are urged to "be mighty men and women of God" and "fight the battles of the Lord" and "do great things for God." We love the idea of being a hero and winning a great battle for God. There's a lot of what we call "glory" in it. But we're not so keen on laying down our lives in the manner of Christ at Calvary. We fail to comprehend the glory of the cross. So we struggle with which model to adopt. The hero or the saint? Achilles or Emmanuel? Caesar or Christ? Charlemagne or St. Francis? More often than not we end up choosing the hero, and this feeds one of the ugliest aspects of a misshapen Christianity—triumphalism.

Triumphalism is an ugly form of arrogance engendering a sense of group superiority. Triumphalism is a smugness and boastful pride that one's nationality or religion is superior to all others. If Christians aren't careful, they can be easily seduced into the ugliness of triumphalism. As Christians we believe that Jesus has triumphed over sin, Satan, death, hell, and the grave. We confess that every knee will bow and every tongue confess that Jesus is Lord.* We call Jesus King of kings and Lord of lords. But this does *not* entitle us to an attitude of arrogant triumphalism. Confessing the triumph of Christ

---

\*   Philippians 2:9–11

should not lead to the ugliness of triumphalism. In fact, the Christian attitude should be the very opposite.

The Christian attitude must be the deep humility exhibited by the apostle Paul when he described himself as "the foremost" of sinners.* Paul was able to boldly confess the lordship of Christ while at the same time exhibiting an attitude that was completely devoid of arrogance and triumphalism. In the pluralistic cultures of the modern Western world, the ugliness of triumphalism will prevent multitudes of people from seeing the true beauty of Christianity. If we engage with people of other faiths with the attitude equivalent to "my religious founder can beat up your religious founder," we should not be surprised if they do not see the Christian faith as inherently beautiful.

A continual turning to the cruciform leaves no room for triumphalism. Yes, Jesus triumphed over evil, but he did so by the counterintuitive way of humbling himself to the point of death, "even death on a cross."† As we seek to assimilate the cruciform into our lives, it should always produce the beauty of a graceful humility and never the ugliness of arrogant triumphalism. If we are to show forth the beauty of Christ in our world, we must banish triumphalist attitudes from among us. It was the attitude of triumphalism in the Middle Ages that led to the ugly actions of the Crusades. Since Jesus had triumphed through the cross, it was reasoned, why not help spread his triumph through the conquest of the sword? The Crusades were the ugly offspring of a union of power-obsessed pragmatism and arrogant religious triumphalism, and I fear

---

* 1 Timothy 1:15
† Philippians 2:8

that this kind of distorted thinking may have certain modern equivalents.

One more thought on heroes and saints. Heroes tend to be heroes to only one side—*their* side. Heroes attain their glory in an "us versus them" context. For example, the French and the Russians have decidedly different views of Napoleon, just as Americans and Mexicans will view Santa Anna differently. But saints, over time, tend to be universally recognized for their saintliness. It has to do with the universality of love. It's why nearly everyone admires St. Francis of Assisi or Mother Teresa of Calcutta whether or not they are Christian. St. Francis and Mother Teresa are preeminent examples of lives shaped by the cruciform to a degree that their lives of co-suffering love have come to be universally recognized as lives of beauty.

So in the present situation in which the American evangelical church finds itself, there is a desperate need to recover a theology of beauty. The way out of the mess and confusion of a politicized faith is to follow the path of beauty. It is the way of beauty that will lead us home to a more authentic Christianity. A theology of beauty is the antidote to the poison of pragmatism and the toxin of triumphalism. Perhaps no other theologian has done as much to develop a theology of beauty as the great Swiss theologian Hans Urs von Balthasar. In his work on love as form and beauty he writes:

> Love alone is credible; nothing else can be believed, and nothing else ought to be believed. This is the achievement, the "work" of faith...to believe that there is such a thing as love...and that there is nothing higher or greater than it....The first thing that must strike a non-Christian about the Christian's faith is that...it is obviously too good to be true: the

mystery of being, revealed as absolute love, condescending to wash his creatures' feet, and even their souls, taking upon himself all the confusion of guilt, all the God-directed hatred, all the accusations showered upon him with cudgels...all the mocking hostility...in order to pardon his creature....This is truly too much.[10]

Indeed, it is too much! The apostle Paul would describe this extravagance as "the love of Christ that surpasses knowledge."* The picture of God as seen in the redemptive co-suffering love of Christ is too much in the sense that it overwhelms us in much the same way that we find a stunning sculpture, a masterpiece painting, or a majestic sunset overwhelming—it is the experience of being overawed by a transcendent beauty. This is how the gospel is made most compelling—by making it beautiful. Instead of trying to overwhelm a cynical world weary of argument and suspicious of truth claims with the force of logic and debate, what if they were overwhelmed with the perception and persuasion of beauty?

Beauty is graceful and has a way of sneaking past our defenses. It's hard to argue with beauty. Beauty is compelling in its own way. What I am suggesting is that we look to beauty as a primary standard for our theology, witness, and action. As radical as it may sound to those who have grown up in the sterile world of late modernity, asking the question *Is it beautiful?* is a valid and viable way to evaluate what we believe and do. We should ask ourselves: "Is this a beautiful doctrine?" "Is this a beautiful witness?" "Is this a beautiful practice?" Along with asking if it is true and if it is good, we should also ask if is it beautiful. Truth and goodness need

---

* Ephesians 3:19

beauty. Truth claims divorced from beauty can become condescending. Goodness minus beauty can become moralistic. To embrace truth and goodness in the Christian sense, we must also embrace beauty.

At least as far back as the Greek philosopher Plato, beauty was understood not merely as an adornment, but as a value as important as truth and goodness. It was only in the twentieth century that beauty began to be diminished as a value. Now we live in a day when pragmatism and utilitarian "values" have largely displaced beauty as a value. But the loss of beauty as a principal value has been disastrous for Western culture. One obvious example of what has befallen us is the loss of aesthetic sensibilities in architecture. Where once the role of architecture was to help beautify the shared space of our cities and neighborhoods, now the role of architecture is to build utilitarian structures as cheaply as possible. The result has been a profound loss of beauty. It's a kind of vandalism. What modern building would people a thousand years from now flock to visit as we do the Notre Dame Cathedral today? If the Gothic cathedral was the architectural statement of the Middle Ages, the "big box" store may well be the architectural statement of our age. This is tragic. But what if what has happened to architecture is also happening to Christianity? What if modern architecture mirrors what is happening in modern Christianity? What if utility is triumphing over beauty in the way we think about the church? This is alarming.

As our world turns its back on beauty, the result is that we are increasingly surrounded by ugliness and images of alienation. Think of government housing projects and the soulless strip malls of suburbia. Art itself is under assault. Art is now largely driven, not by time-tested standards of beauty, but by the marketplace. So the question is no longer, "Is it beautiful?," but "Will it sell?" (Is this too reflected in the church?) In a world where kitsch, profit, and vulgarity are vandalizing art, philosopher Roger Scruton worries that we are in danger of losing beauty, and with it the meaning of life.[11] Yes, the loss of beauty is related to the loss of meaning. Attaining to the beautiful is a valid way of understanding the meaning of life—especially when we recognize a link between the sacred and the beautiful. For thousands of years, artists, sages, philosophers, and theologians have connected the beautiful and the sacred and identified art with our longing for God. It has only been during the modern phenomenon of secularism—what Nietzsche described as the "death of God"—that we have severed the beautiful from the divine. But when the beautiful is severed from the absolute (God), what passes for beautiful can be anything and everything—which is to say nothing. There really is a profound connection between the loss of beauty and the loss of meaning.

Yet despite the modern assault upon art and beauty, the hunger for beauty abides deep in the human heart. That the allure of beauty is part of the human makeup is clearly seen every time a child picks up crayons and tries to capture the beauty of the world around him. And it is to this firmly entrenched desire for beauty that we should appeal in our efforts to communicate the gospel. If we can show a world lost in the ugliness of consumer-driven pragmatism and power-hungry politics the true beauty of Christ, it will be irresistibly appealing. For too long we have relied upon the cold logic of apologetics to persuade or the crass techniques of the marketplace to entice, when what we should do is creatively hold forth the transcendent beauty of Jesus Christ. But to do this, we must examine what we preach and what we practice in the light of the beauty of the cruciform.

We need to constantly ask ourselves, "Is this beautiful? Is this thought beautiful? Is the attitude beautiful? Is this action beautiful? Does it reflect the beauty of Christ and the cruciform?" If finger-pointing isn't beautiful, then we should abandon it. If politically based protest isn't beautiful, then maybe we can do without it. If the common man doesn't recognize what we do in the name of Christ as beautiful, we should at least reexamine it. If a particular doctrine doesn't come across as truly beautiful, then we should hold it suspect. Someone may raise the question, "Can beauty be trusted?" I believe it can, as long as we make the critical distinction between the shallow and faddish thing that our modern culture calls "image" and the absolute value that our ancestors have always understood as beauty. We can rightly evaluate our faith and practice in terms of beauty for this very reason: The Lord and his ways are beautiful. "He has made everything beautiful in its time."*

It's time to recover the form and beauty of Christianity. Our enduring icon of beauty and the standard by which we gauge the beauty of our actions is the cruciform. The cross is a beautiful mystery—a mystery where an unexpected beauty is in the process of rescuing the world from its ugliness. Beauty *will* save the world. This is the surprising beauty of the cross when seen through the prism of the resurrection. The cross made beautiful is the ultimate triumph of God and his grace. If the crucifixion of Christ can be made beautiful, then there is hope that all the ugliness of the human condition can be redeemed by its beauty.

---

* Ecclesiastes 3:11, ESV

## CHAPTER 2

# THE GREATEST
# WONDER OF ALL

BEAUTY. MYSTERY. WONDER. They all three go together. The primary human response to an encounter with overwhelming beauty is wonder. Wonder is the transcendent sensation we experience when we find ourselves in the presence of an awe-inspiring sunset, an artistic masterpiece, or a newborn baby. Wonder is the uniquely human reaction to the sublime. Cows and cats don't wonder, but humans do. Wonder is a large part of what it means to be human. Wonder defined is, "a feeling of surprise mingled with admiration caused by something beautiful, unexpected, or inexplicable."[1] We wonder at two things—the beautiful and the mysterious. A life stripped of beauty and mystery is a life barren of wonder, and a life without wonder is a kind of deep poverty.

Children inhabit a magical world rich in beauty and replete with wonder. It's children who find their way to the wonderfilled world of Narnia in C. S. Lewis's classic series The

Chronicles of Narnia. A healthy and happy childhood spills over with wonder, for the simple reason that through the eyes of a child, beauty is abundant and mystery is everywhere. A ladybug on a leaf, a puddle in the street, an unexplored closet, the moon in the sky at night—they all have more than enough beauty and mystery to evoke wonder. For a child, his own backyard and a little imagination are sufficient for hours of wonder...until he grows up. Then the wonder is gone, and the backyard becomes little more than a lawn to be mowed. The tragedy of growing up is not that we put aside childishness, but that we lose the capacity for childlike wonder. As children we dream of finding our own real-life adventure...and we end up finding a job. Adventure is set aside for a career and wonder is the casualty. As children we are in a hurry to grow up because we believe the possibilities of life are limitless, and it is only the strictures of childhood that hold us back. But then we make the deflating discovery that with the freedom of growing up come the responsibilities of adulthood. We also discover that with the loss of childhood comes the loss of wonder. And we miss it terribly. Perhaps more than we know.

The loss of wonder is what we experience as boredom, and boredom is a real problem. Despite what we may think, boredom is not a trivial thing—it is a killer. The Danish philosopher and religious thinker Søren Kierkegaard said, "Boredom is a root of all evil."[2] I know what Kierkegaard means by that, and I agree. Boredom *is* dangerous and deadly. But in what way? Wonder is a feeling. Boredom is the loss of such feeling. Sometimes we're led to believe that feelings are unimportant, and I suppose that's true for a machine, but we're not machines. (Part of the collateral damage of the Industrial Revolution is our modern tendency to objectify and mechanize everything, including people.) People devoid of human sensation and passionate feeling will often engage in dangerous and destructive actions in a desperate bid to feel something. Behind the evils of addiction and many other forms of self-destructive behavior lies the culprit of boredom.

We can think of boredom as a kind of disease, a leprosy of the soul—and leprosy is not what you assume it is. Contrary to what most people imagine, leprosy is not a disease that eats away the flesh of the victim. Rather, leprosy is simply nerve damage. Leprosy destroys the capacity to feel. Leprosy is numbness. And that may not seem like much, but all the damage that disfigures the leper (and I've seen many lepers in India)—the missing fingers, the marred faces, the open sores—is self-inflicted damage. The truth is the leper hurts himself because he has lost the capacity to feel. Numbness is indeed dangerous—a root of all kinds of evil. What leprosy is to the physical nervous system, boredom is to the soul. Thus people who are deeply bored can inflict a lot of damage on themselves as they attempt to once again feel something. It's what Trent Reznor talks about in his song "Hurt"—a deeply poignant song about addiction, made famous by Johnny Cash. "Hurt" is a kind of requiem about the loss and pain we bring upon our lives and the lives of those around us when we've lost the capacity to feel. Wonder gone. Feeling lost. It's a dangerous situation. How much addiction is a toxic attempt to recapture lost wonder? How much reckless living is a dangerous bid to compensate for the creeping numbness of adulthood? It's a valid question.

Years before Johnny Cash made "Hurt" famous, Pink Floyd recorded their song "Comfortably Numb" along a similar theme—we grow up, lose wonder, and settle for being comfortably numb; but it's really a kind of death. So we should never again say feelings don't matter—they do matter. Wonder is a feeling. An essential feeling. The loss of wonder is the loss of feeling. And when we lose the feeling of wonder, life just gets hard. The simple act of growing up and leaving child-hood behind shouldn't be such a catastrophe for our ability to wonder and be enchanted by mystery and beauty, but it seems that it is. It is this loss of childlike wonder and imagination that Austrian artist Gottfried Helnwein decries in his bom-bastic style when he says:

> I always felt so much more comfortable communicating with children than with grown-ups. Everything is far more simple and makes so much more sense—to me at least. In the world of a child anything is possible, there are no limits for the imagination, and magic and miracles are a natural part of it—art and life are one. Communicating with adults, on the other hand, sometimes seems to be so limited and incredibly com-plicated and above all boring. Unfortunately it's the grown-ups that rule the world and make the laws and all kids have to go through their training-program called education....Funnily enough it doesn't always work. Some kids seem to be relatively immune to the program, and one day I realized: that's what almost all artists have in common—to a certain degree they all managed to continue being a child.[3]

Helnwein makes a valid point about art. Art is often an attempt to recapture the wonder that is in the world when seen through the eyes of innocence, the eyes of a child. Wonder is so much more than empty amusement or an evening's enter-tainment. Wonder is an essential ingredient if life is to be made livable. Wonder is the cure—the cure for life-killing boredom. Wonder is the drug—the natural drug without which people may turn to narcotic drugs. Sure, most people bravely soldier on without wonder, and even do so without drug addictions and self-destructive behavior. But is that the point of life? To soldier on after the thrill of living is gone? That's not life—that's life with all the wonder crushed out of it and compressed to mere existence. Wonder is what we've lost. Wonder is what we miss. Wonder is what we want. "It [wonder] is our hidden Narnia into which we long to step and explore."[4]

A few years ago I was thinking about these things while on a family vacation in the Rocky Mountains. During our long hikes I would muse on the role of wonder in finding satisfaction in life. One evening I found myself alone at sundown in the high country on a ridge well above the tree line. A thunderstorm had passed through a little earlier and was now rumbling off to the east. What was before me as I looked to the west was a masterpiece sunset over the Never Summer Mountains. I wanted to thoroughly absorb the beauty that was on full display before me, so I sat down on the alpine tundra in that numinous world that one naturalist describes as "a land of contrast and incredible intensity, where the sky is the size of forever and the flowers are the size of a millisecond."[5] I remained in solitude until I was joined by seven bull elk, which ambled up the ridge to where I was sitting. As the elk grazed, they were aware of my presence but entirely unconcerned. Then, just as the orange orb of the sun was touching the snowcapped peaks of the Never Summer Mountains, the largest of the elk drew closer, looked at me, and then lifted his head in such a way that his massive antlers formed a perfect frame for the majestic sunset in the distance. It was an encounter with such rare beauty that I can only describe it as sacred. Wonder rushed into my soul, and I felt the full thrill of being alive. I prayed: "God, I want to live my whole life in a constant state of wonder." Then God spoke to me.

In saying "God spoke to me," I realize that such claims can be made in a reckless manner, and I try to avoid labeling my own thoughts and ideas as the voice of God—but this really was one of those rare occasions in life where the Infinite breaks through to the finite, and the voice of God is heard by man. It was not a thought from within; it was a Voice from elsewhere. It was a genuine mystical experience. Though not audible, the Voice was as distinct and real as the rolling thunder I could still hear in the distance. The Voice said: "This is the greatest wonder of all—the Word became flesh and dwelt among us."

At the risk of sounding cliché, I can only say that that moment at sundown in the Rocky Mountains was a significant turning point in my life. It was as if God had given me a golden key—the key to wonder. That key was the mystery of the Incarnation—the mystery of the Word made flesh, the greatest wonder of all. I couldn't stop thinking about it. As I traveled for speaking engagements in other churches, I would bypass the regular chit-chat on church affairs with the host pastor and launch into my new favorite topic of discussion with a direct question: "So, what do you think about the Incarnation?" (Sadly, I found that not nearly enough pastors are actually interested in theological conversation.) Over time I have become obsessed with the sacred mystery of the Incarnation, and it is a magnificent obsession indeed. To think deeply about the Incarnation is sacred meditation. I have pondered long over the apostle John's poetic prologue to his

Gospel memoir. Allow me to reproduce John's introductory poem in poetic form (with the narrative portions omitted).

> In the beginning was the Word,
>   and the Word was with God,
>   and the Word was God.
> He was in the beginning with God.
> All things came into being through him,
>   and without him not one thing came into being.
> What has come into being in him was life,
>   and the life was the light of all people.
> The light shines in the darkness,
>   and the darkness did not overcome it.
> The true light,
>   which enlightens everyone,
>   was coming into the world.
> He was in the world,
>   and the world came into being through him;
>   yet the world did not know him.
> He came to what was his own,
>   and his own people did not accept him.
> But to all who received him,
>   who believed in his name,
>   he gave power to become children of God,
>   who were born,
>   not of blood
>   or of the will of the flesh
>   or of the will of man,
>   but of God.
> And the Word became flesh and lived among us,
>   and we have seen his glory,
>   the glory as of a father's only son,
>   full of grace and truth.
> From his fullness we have all received,
>   grace upon grace.
> The law indeed was given through Moses;
>   grace and truth came through Jesus Christ.

No one has ever seen God.
It is God the only Son,
  who is close to the Father's heart,
  who has made him known.

                        —JOHN 1:1–5, 9–14, 16–18

There are some mysteries so transcendent, so sacred, so otherworldly, that they cannot be adequately communicated in prose; only poetry will do. The Incarnation is one of those mysteries. This is why the apostle John opens his Gospel with a poetic meditation upon the Incarnation. What follows the prologue is John's unique telling of the Jesus story. John's Gospel (quite different from Matthew, Mark, and Luke) is like a vortex, a whirlpool, that, if we fall into it—and the best way to read the Gospels is to fall into the story—we find ourselves drawn to a single focal point. That focal point is this: Jesus is the full revelation of God. Jesus is the eternal Word of God made human flesh. Truly this is the greatest wonder of all. The wonder we long for is found in the sacred mysteries of the faith, and a return to these mysteries can recapture the wonder. Recapturing wonder is part of salvation. We become jaded and bored because we mistakenly think there are no more mysteries to imbue us with wonder, but the Incarnation is an eternal fountain of mystery and wonder. In the mystery and wonder of the Incarnation is found the beauty that saves the world.

Consider the apostle John's great confession concerning the Incarnation—"The Word became flesh." By which is meant the *Logos*, the Word, the Idea, the Reason, the Reflection, the Meditation, the Self-Understanding of GOD became flesh, became human flesh and blood! Simply put, God became one of us. But do we really believe that? Yes, as an article of faith, if we are orthodox in our Christianity, we confess that Jesus Christ is fully God and fully human. But have we dared to really meditate on the mysterious and wonder-inducing implications of God becoming *one of us*?

In 1995 Joan Osborne recorded the hit song "One of Us." The song is a kind of secular but serious meditation on what it would be like if God was one of us. It muses about God as a stranger, riding a bus, blending into the crowd, and what the implications are in believing in God becoming so utterly human that he could be overlooked and ignored.

At the time the song generated controversy, especially among certain Christian groups who found the song offensive. (There are some Christians who see it as their task in life to be regularly offended at something!) But I like the song. What if God was one of us? What a great question! Because as Christians we confess that God *has* become one of us—this is the mystery and wonder of the Incarnation. And this mystery deserves serious thought and meditation. The offense with Joan Osborne's song lies mostly in the fact that it is a far more honest exploration of the Incarnation than most Christians are comfortable with or are willing to engage in.

The nature of the Incarnation is that it *is* scandalous and it *is* offensive. It was the offense and scandalous nature of the Incarnation that led to the early Christian heresies of Gnosticism, Docetism, Arianism, and others. Some were scandalized by the very idea that God could and would become one of us. So they tried to diminish either the full divinity of Christ (Arianism) or the full humanity of Christ (Gnosticism and Docetism). But the church was resolute in its confession of the "hypostatic union"—that Jesus Christ is fully human and fully God, possessing both realities in one person. As a matter of doctrine, the question of Christ's full humanity was settled seventeen centuries ago, but we still must learn to take seriously the implications of the Incarnation. Failure to do so leads to a cheap, sentimental, cartoon Christianity. Hans Urs von Balthasar says:

> All the kitsch to be found in the Christian life and Christian art arises from a failure to take it [the humanity of Christ] seriously.[6]

Kitsch is cheap, imitative, sentimental art done in poor taste. (Think of "Precious Moments" religious art.) Kitsch is a parody of beauty and a mockery of mystery. A kind of kitsch Christianity is what we are left with if we don't take the Incarnation seriously. If we don't deeply contemplate the absolute and full humanity of Christ, and if we don't work the Incarnation thoroughly into our thinking and theology, we end up with a cartoon Christ, a "Precious Moments" parody, or Jesus as one of the "Super Friends"—a comic book hero who is thoroughly unbelievable. This is Gnosticism in one of its more common forms.

If we think of Jesus during his three-year ministry as Superman flying around being God all over the place, we get Jesus wrong and do a disservice to the mystery of the Incarnation. Yes, Jesus was fully God, but he was also fully human, and his divinity did not obliterate his humanity. Jesus's humanity was not a costume or a disguise; it was his true identity. Jesus's divinity was enfleshed in a genuine and authentic humanity. Everyone who encountered Jesus of Nazareth regarded him as fully human. This is evidenced by the fact that Jesus's own brothers, though they doubtless regarded their brother as a righteous man, did not believe he was the Messiah, much less that he was God.* Jesus's brothers did not believe he was anything other than human until after his resurrection. Of course Jesus did miracles—seven miracles are specifically recorded in the Gospel of John to witness to the divinity of Christ—but these miracles flowed *through* Jesus's humanity; they did not bypass his humanity. So we do not disavow the full humanity of Christ when we confess his divinity. This is the sacred mystery, the greatest wonder of all, that the Word of God eternally begotten from the Father became flesh—not as a mere garment, but in true being. The Word *became* flesh, human flesh. Flesh subject to disease, aging, and death. We know that Jesus was subject to death, for he did die. He was also aging. When he was not yet thirty-five people described him as "not yet fifty."† We would hardly take that as a compliment! What about disease? Was Jesus subject to childhood diseases like the rest of us? I assume so. John tells us that Jesus's first miracle was to turn water into wine at Cana of Galilee, not the miracle of supernatural immunity to childhood diseases. Yes, Jesus was God, but his humanity was derived from his mother, and as such his physical body was subject to the same limits and duress as our own. But I have noticed that even seventeen centuries following the Council of Nicaea and the confession that Christ is fully human, many modern Christians still hold to vestiges of Docetism, believing that somehow Jesus only *seemed* to be fully human. They simply find it difficult to believe that in Christ God really became one of us.

But God *did* join humanity in the Incarnation. So that God is born, God grows, and God learns. We can tremble at the

---

* John 7:5
† John 8:57

*Christ the second Adam*

mysterious paradox of how the eternal can be born, and how omnipotence can grow, and how omniscience can learn...but we dare not deny it. As Jesus comes into manhood, we find the God who labors, the God who sweats, the God who sleeps. Because Jesus ate and drank, labored and rested, sorrowed and celebrated, all these human experiences are conferred a kind of sanctity. In the Incarnation Jesus makes beautiful all that it means to be human. The incarnation of Christ as a common laborer makes sacred the whole spectrum of human vocation.

*Mary the second Eve*

Christ assumed humanness in order to redeem humanness, and the Incarnation lies at the very heart of God's redemptive agenda. One way of understanding the Old Testament is that it tells the story of the long journey toward what the apostle Paul called "the fullness of time" when the Son of God was "born of a woman."* As the Orthodox theologian Vladimir Lossky said:

*"Be it unto me as you have said" free will*

> All the sacred tradition of the Jews is a history of the slow and laborious journey of fallen humanity towards the "fullness of time" when the angel was to be sent to announce to the chosen Virgin the Incarnation of God and to hear from her lips human consent, so that the divine plan might be accomplished.[7]

Nothing that belongs essentially to the human experience was exempted in the Incarnation, except sin—which is what Christ came to save us from. So in Christ God is born, God grows, God learns, God labors, God sweats, God sleeps. Finally in Christ we find a God who weeps, a God who suffers, and, most astonishingly of all, a God who dies! Whatever it means for a human being to experience death,

---

* Galatians 4:4

God in Christ has experienced. This is the sacred mystery of Holy Saturday. In his critique of religion, Nietzsche's madman famously announces: "God is dead." But four and a half centuries before Nietzsche's provocative use of that term, Martin Luther composed a Holy Saturday hymn entitled, "God Is Dead." Why? Because before we confess that "on the third day he rose again," we first confess that Christ "was crucified, died, and was buried." The very reason we can be saved from death is that God in Christ fully entered into death. Christ descended into death that he might lead the way out. The beauty that saves the world occurs through the ugliness of death. Theologian Aidan Nichols says it like this:

> The Incarnation is the divine means of transfiguring the world into greater beauty precisely by redeeming the divine image in man from the deformity of sin.... All saving history leads up to the Incarnation or issues from it.[8]

The lost beauty of God's good creation is what is recovered in the Incarnation. The beauty of the image of God marred in man through the Fall is what the Incarnation redeems. By a deep appreciation of the human vocation to bear the image of God, we realize that the value of a human being is in no way determined by what he can do—this is the sin of objectification (treating humans as objects). Human value is derived from the image all humans bear—the *Imago Dei*. It is the image of God deformed in humanity that Christ recovers through his Incarnation.

Think of the Transfiguration—that mystical event when Jesus took Peter, James, and John to a high mountain and, while praying, was "transfigured beforse them, and his face shone like the sun, and his clothes became dazzling white."* The Transfiguration is a prophecy of what God intends for creation in Christ, so that "the earth will be filled with the knowledge of the glory of the Lord, as the waters cover the sea."† It is through the Incarnation that glory and beauty save the world.

Hans Urs von Balthasar gives us a marvelous illustration of how the Incarnation brings salvation into the world. Think of an hourglass. Two glass spheres; one full, the other empty. But they are connected *at a single point*. It is at this single point that the fullness of one sphere flows into the emptiness of the other sphere. Jesus Christ as God and man is the single point where the sphere of divinity and the sphere of humanity connect. It is what we mean when we say that Jesus Christ is fully human and fully God. It is through the single point of connection between the two spheres that emptiness becomes fullness. As the apostle John says, "From his fullness we have all received, grace upon grace."‡

The limitation of the hourglass illustration is that the contents in the upper (heavenly) sphere are finite, and in time (presumably an hour) it will be emptied. But the heavenly sphere of the divine is infinite and eternal, so that as God pours himself into humanity through the singularity of Christ, we receive fullness, while God is never diminished. As Gregory the Great said in the sixth century, "In the mystery of the Incarnation God increases what is ours, without diminishing what is his."[9] What is it that is poured into humanity through the connecting point of the Incarnation? Life—eternal life! To

---

* Matthew 17:2
† Habakkuk 2:14
‡ John 1:16

believe on Jesus Christ is to connect with the point at which divine grace and eternal life are poured by God into humanity. What a beautiful and sacred mystery!

Through the Incarnation, the Word of God came into the world to bring the world light and life—the light and life that is salvation. But there was also a great darkness, a malevolent darkness, a darkness that ruled the world, a darkness that kept humanity enslaved to death. The light that was coming into the world would be challenged by this darkness.

> In him was life, and the life was the light of all people. The light shines in the darkness and the darkness did not overcome it.... The true light, which enlightens everyone, was coming into the world.
>
> —JOHN 1:4–5, 9

The prophet Isaiah spoke of a light that would dawn in the darkened land of Galilee—a land frequently dominated by pagan Gentile powers, so that it was called Galilee of the Gentiles (or nations).

> But there will be no more gloom for those who were in anguish. In the former time he brought into contempt the land of Zebulun and the land of Naphtali, but in the latter time he will make glorious the way of the sea, the land beyond the Jordan, Galilee of the nations.
>
> The people who walked in darkness
>   have seen a great light;
> those who lived in a land of deep darkness—
>   on them light has shined.
>
> —ISAIAH 9:1–2

Humanity had long languished in darkness—the darkness of sin and death, violence and war, ignorance and superstition. But now the light of God was at last coming into the world. It would dawn in Galilee—a land shared (though not always peacefully) by Jews and Gentiles. The northern territory of Galilee allotted to Zebulun and Naphtali was lightly regarded. It was thought of as backward, provincial, unenlightened. Galilee was not the region of the elites; it was "fly over country." But it was in Galilee that the light of God first began to shine. How? Through a human life. The light of God was a *life*—a human life—a life that would show us two interconnected things that we did not know: what God is like and how to be human. To get the latter right, we must first get the former right. True worship forms us into the image of God. Idolatry, on the other hand, is the practice of forming God into our own image. But to avoid the seduction of idolatry, we need to be able to clearly see God.

It's true that the Jewish people shared a special relationship with God because of their Messianic vocation, and, as a result, they had been given a certain revelatory perspective of God. The patriarchs received divine visitations. Moses received the divine Law. The prophets received divine oracles. All of this gave Israel a definite inside track on the understanding of God. Nevertheless, John is quite clear when he says, "No one has ever seen God."* John is emphatic—despite the various experiences, visions, and revelations of Old Testament Israel, God remained unseen. John then reveals the great implication of the Word made flesh when he says, "It is God the only Son, who is close to the Father's heart, who has made him

---

* John 1:18

known."* The Incarnation shows us what we could never have seen otherwise. Despite the experiences of Abraham, Moses, David, and the prophets, God was still not truly seen or fully known. It had been hints and guesses in the dark. But now light would shine, and God would be known in the person of Jesus Christ! The light of revelation would emanate from the startling sermons Jesus of Nazareth first preached in the hills of Galilee. Jesus was showing us God and showing us how to be human.

At the end of his public ministry, on the night of his betrayal, Jesus would make the boldest claim of all to his disciples: "Whoever has seen me has seen the Father."† Now if we want to know what God is like, we look, not to Moses, not to Joshua, not to David, not to Elijah—but to Jesus! The Old Testament saints give us partial glimpses of the divine, but the full revelation of God is found only in Christ. This is the unique Christian confession concerning Christ—that Jesus is God, and to see Jesus is to see God in human form. Likewise, it is in looking to Jesus Christ that we understand how to be human—how to be human in a way that is not dominated by darkness and destructive to ourselves and others. It is in believing that Jesus is the light of the world and following his pattern of life that we live in the light and become what Jesus called "children of light."‡ This is the way back to beauty. The Septuagint (the Greek Translation of the Hebrew Scriptures) translates Genesis 1:4 as: "And God saw that the light was beautiful." Jesus as the light of the world is the beauty of God coming into the world.

---

\* John 1:18
† John 14:9
‡ John 12:36

But as the light of Christ came into the world, the darkness did not remain passive. The darkness challenged the light. The darkness tested this unique life. The darkness tempted the human life that was the light of the world. Jesus encountered the challenge of the darkness most powerfully in the wilderness temptation. In a series of ingenious temptations, Satan attempted to lure Jesus over to "the dark side" (to cast it in terms of a familiar literary theme). Matthew, Mark, and Luke all refer to the wilderness temptation of Christ early in their Gospels (Mark in passing, Matthew and Luke in detail). John refers to the temptation as well, but he does it in his poetic way when he writes, "The light shines in the darkness, and the darkness did not overcome it."* It is right here, in considering the temptation of Christ, that we must keep the full humanity of Christ before us, for if we don't, the whole thing degenerates into a trite and cartoonish parody; it collapses into kitsch. If we imagine the devil showing up sporting horns and a tail and toting a pitchfork while trying to play *Let's Make a Deal* with Jesus, the temptation isn't real; it's merely a satire of temptation. Jesus faced a *real* temptation; Jesus was genuinely tempted. How are we to understand this?

Pg. 42

Following his baptism, Jesus was led by the Holy Spirit into the Judean wilderness where he spent forty days in prayer and fasting. He is about to begin his public ministry, and presumably during these forty days Jesus is contemplating the course he is about to take. In other words, we can safely say Jesus was thinking about how he was going to go about the work of Messiah. At the end of these forty days, we are told the devil came to him with three temptations. But how did the devil

---

* John 1:5

come? Not as an overt creature clearly distinct from Jesus—for then there would be virtually no temptation. Satan didn't come strolling across the wilderness and say, "Hello, I'm the devil. I'm here to tempt you. Where shall we start?" No, the darkness is much more subtle than that. I'm certain the temptation came to Christ in the same way it comes to all of us—in the form of dark thoughts that somehow enter our mind, thoughts that we don't always immediately recognize as originating with the powers of darkness. As Jesus contemplates how to go about his messianic mission, Satan offered Jesus three dark alternatives. And each of these dark alternatives was tempting to Jesus. The dark trilogy of satanic temptations was the enticements of bread, circuses, and empire. We might also think of them as the temptations of prosperity, popularity, and politics.

At the end of his forty-day fast, Jesus was first tempted by the devil to turn stones into bread. Was this merely a temptation to satisfy legitimate hunger at the end of a long fast by an illegitimate employment of miraculous means? I think much more is implied here. Jesus is thinking about the ministry he is about to begin. How should he go about it? How should he get people to follow him? Ah, here's a thought—base it on meeting people's material needs. Meet people's most "felt" needs, as we say. After all, supplying people with bread has long been a common path to power. Give people what they want; that's the ticket. They want bread, they need bread, so supply them with it. It seems like a good idea…for a moment. But then Jesus detects the darkness in the idea and replies, "Man shall not live by bread alone, but by every word that comes from the mouth of God."* This temptation is brilliant for its subtlety (and the devil is nothing if not subtle). Bread is good. Giving people bread is good. But the idea that all man needs for a meaningful existence is enough bread is *not* good. People are too prone to sell their souls for a morsel of bread, and thus they are easily manipulated. Jesus would not cooperate with the secular solution of meeting merely material need. Blaise Pascal was right; there is something like a God-shaped hole in the heart of man. "This infinite abyss can be filled only with an infinite and immutable object; in other words by God Himself."[10] Bread alone will not suffice.

Later Jesus did supply bread for people, but on his own terms. Through the miracle of the multiplication of the loaves and fishes, Jesus fed five thousand. But what happened? The people came to take Jesus by force and make him king. Jesus responded by withdrawing and hiding himself.† We need to think this through. Jesus *was* king. Jesus came to be king. *Messiah* meant king. But when the people tried to make Jesus king, he declined. Why? Jesus had already addressed that temptation in the wilderness—he would not be made king for the wrong reason, and a miraculous supply of bread was the wrong reason to be made king. So the next day when people asked for Jesus to again supply them with bread, all Jesus offered them was his flesh to eat and his blood to drink. They called him crazy, and all but his most devoted disciples stopped following him.‡ Jesus had resisted the dark temptation to build his kingdom around the promise of material prosperity.

---

*  Matthew 4:4, ESV
†  See John 6:15.
‡  See John 6:22–71.

In the second temptation Jesus thinks about another way to gain a following. He imagines himself on the pinnacle of the temple in Jerusalem. When a large crowd was gathered—perhaps during one of the festivals—he could leap from the temple in the sight of all and then be caught mid-fall by angels in an overawing display of divinity. After all, the Scriptures promise angelic protection for the righteous. But Jesus sees the temptation for what it is and responds, "Again it is written, 'Do not put the Lord your God to the test.'"* Jesus saw the temptation of the pinnacle as tantamount to making God prove himself. So he rejects it. And this at least goes some of the way in addressing the vexing question, Why isn't God more obvious? Couldn't God overwhelmingly convince every atheist, agnostic, and skeptic of the reality of his existence? Couldn't God just "prove" himself and make atheism impossible? We would suppose so. But if God were to do so, it would undermine his intention to have authentic beings who bear his image. It would make God no more than a skillful puppet master of human marionettes. As C. S. Lewis said:

> The Irresistible and the Indisputable are the two weapons which the very nature of His scheme forbids Him to use. Merely to override a human will (as His felt presence in any but the faintest and most mitigated degree would certainly do) would be for Him useless. He cannot ravish. He can only woo.[11]

Likewise, Dostoevsky spoke of God's "miracle of restraint,"[12] and Kierkegaard talked about "God's light touch."[13] Jesus would not override the miracle of restraint and God's light touch by the empirical proof of a leap from the pinnacle. Belief

---

\* Matthew 4:7

in Christ would require a leap to faith. Jesus had not come to capture but to liberate, and thus he rejected the second temptation to turn the kingdom of God into a circus of the sensational. The saving faith would be founded on one essential sign—the resurrection sign of Jonah. Jesus rejected the lust for more signs and proofs as coming from the evil one, for he said to those who demanded a miraculous sign, "An evil and adulterous generation asks for a sign, but no sign will be given to it except the sign of the prophet Jonah. For just as Jonah was three days and three nights in the belly of the sea monster, so for three days and three nights the Son of Man will be in the heart of the earth."* The resurrection would be Christ's only proof of validity. Jesus would not do circus tricks on command in order to obtain a following.

> "Free as a bird," we say, and envy the winged creatures for their unrestricted power of movement in all the three dimensions. But, alas, we forget the dodo. Any bird that has learned to grub up a good living without being compelled to use its wings will soon renounce the privilege of flight and remain forever grounded. Something analogous is true of human beings. If bread is supplied regularly and copiously three times a day, many of them will be perfectly content to live by bread alone—or at least by bread and circuses alone.[14]

Jesus would not clip the wings of authentic human freedom by seducing the race of men with bread and circuses. Yes, Jesus would build a movement around himself, but not by the dubious means of what the Roman poet Juvenal called *"panem et circenses."*[15] These tempting shortcuts were rejected. Bread

---

* Matthew 12:39–40

and circuses were the tricks of empire, and Jesus would not adopt them.

But there yet remained the third temptation—the most seductive of all—the temptation of empire itself. Jesus was shown "the kingdoms of the world and their splendor" and an offer was made: "All these I will give you, if you will fall down and worship me."* How are we to understand this temptation? Are we to seriously think Jesus was tempted to become a Satanist engaging in occult worship? No, it was not as crass as that. As with the other two temptations, it was deceptively subtle. As Jesus contemplated how to go about establishing the kingdom of God—for this was the mission of Messiah—the ever-present temptation was to do it in the way of the pharaohs and Caesars. Of course Jesus would be far more righteous than the Egyptian and Roman kings—he would use his kingly power for good, but he would first have to become a king. And this was the temptation, to become a king in the way of kings. It was the temptation to bypass the way of the suffering servant and seize the throne through the will to power. The temptation that constantly presented itself to Jesus was to become a righteous king through the anticipated and accepted, but ultimately unrighteous, means of violence.

> Named by angelic imperative for the liberator Joshua, greeted by the magi as liberator-designate, and targeted for massacre by Herod for the same reason, Jesus faced the temptation of violence as no other. Our sources give no information concerning his inclination to covet, steal, bear false witness, or commit adultery. But from the first testing in the desert to the last one in the garden, his unceasing temptation

---

* Matthew 4:8–9

was the plea of the crowds and even of some of his disciples that he should strike out on the path of righteous kingship.[16]

What could Jesus have accomplished if he had set out on the same path to kingship as the pharaohs and Caesars (or even the Israelite kings of old)? Could he have raised an army? Could he have become a great general? Could he have been the second coming of Joshua, David, or Judah Maccabeus? This is what people expected Messiah to do. Could Jesus have led an Israelite army into victorious battle and liberated the Jewish people from Roman oppression? Could Jesus have taken up the sword against Israel's enemies and "beat them fine as dust before the wind"?* No doubt Jesus was capable of all this…and more. Could the miracle-worker of Nazareth have led an army to march upon Rome, overthrow Caesar, and install himself as the new emperor of a new empire? Who could doubt that Jesus was capable of all of this? If Alexander the Great could conquer the world by the time he was thirty-three, so could Jesus of Nazareth. Of course there would be a crucial difference—the motive would always be to achieve righteousness and justice. But… *it would not be the way of God!*

That's when Jesus saw the temptation for what it was—a temptation to bow down to Satan! So Jesus thundered his reply: "Away with you, Satan! for it is written, 'Worship the Lord your God, and serve only him.'"† Jesus saw that justifying the means by the end was nothing less than Satan worship! In Jesus's rejection of utilizing the means of violence to bring about the kingdom of peace, I can't help but be reminded of

---

\* Psalm 18:42, ESV

† Matthew 4:10

how the good wizard Gandalf rejected the ring-bearer Frodo's offer to hand to him the ring of power in J. R. R. Tolkien's *The Fellowship of the Ring.*

> Don't tempt me, Frodo! I dare not take it. Not even to keep it safe. Understand, Frodo, I would use this ring from a desire to do good. But through me it would wield a power too great and terrible to imagine.[17]

*[handwritten margin notes: a break in !!; always = forever; lift up the voice]*

If Jesus had grabbed the ring of power that Satan offered, it would have corrupted even the Christ! Selah. So was Jesus refusing to be a savior, a deliverer, a king? No. Jesus *would* become a king and liberate Israel, Jesus *would* establish the kingdom of God and conquer the world—*but it would be by the cross and not by the sword.* In overcoming Satan's third temptation, Jesus rejected the enticement of the sword. But the temptation would return. When Jesus first announced to his disciples that his path to kingship would ultimately lead to crucifixion, Peter rebuked Jesus, saying, "God forbid it, Lord! This must never happen to you." Jesus's response was swift and decisive. He turned on Peter and said, "Get behind me, Satan! You are a stumbling block to me."* Jesus had already faced that temptation in the wilderness. Now Peter had brought it to Jesus again. And Jesus would face this same temptation a final time in the Garden of Gethsemane. But Jesus never succumbed to the temptation to justify obvious ugly means by a presumed beautiful end. Jesus knew that if the end was to be truly beautiful, the means would have to be beautiful too.

---

* Matthew 16:22–23

## CHAPTER 3

# AXIS OF LOVE

WE ARE ATTEMPTING to look at Christianity through a new lens, the lens of beauty, and we are trying to ask some new questions. When considering Christian faith and practice, we are used to asking, "Is it true?," but we also need to ask the question, "Is it beautiful?"

The ancient Greek philosophers, and later the early church fathers, spoke of three prime virtues: truth, goodness, and beauty. As prime virtues, truth, goodness, and beauty need no further justification—they are their own justification, which is a way of saying that truth, goodness, and beauty don't need to be made practical—they don't have to *do* anything to be of value. The value of a virtue is inherent; we simply choose truth, goodness, and beauty because they are true, good, and beautiful.

Early Christian theologians located the source of these prime virtues as proceeding from God himself—truth, goodness, and beauty are virtues because God is true, good, and beautiful. Thus this trinity of virtues becomes a guide to

Christian living as we seek to *believe* what is true, *be* what is good, and *behold* what is beautiful.

But it is this third virtue, the virtue of beauty, that has been most marginalized in the way we understand and evaluate Christianity. As a result, Christianity has suffered a loss of beauty—a loss that needs to be recovered. With an emphasis on truth, we have tried to make Christianity persuasive (as we should). But we also need a corresponding emphasis on beauty to make Christianity attractive. Christianity should not only persuade with truth, but it should also attract with beauty. Along with Christian apologetics, we need Christian aesthetics. Christianity needs not only to be defended as true—it also needs to be presented as beautiful. Often where truth cannot convince, beauty can entice.

The aesthetic aspect of Christian witness and doctrine needs to be developed, and we do this by focusing on the unique form of Christian beauty. As we have seen, beauty has a form, and what makes a thing beautiful is adherence to the beautiful form. The unique form of Christianity is the cruciform—Christ upon the cross, arms outstretched in offered embrace, forgiving the world its sins. This is the beauty that saves the world, and the symbol of this saving grace is the cross.

That the Roman cross, an instrument of physical torture and psychological terror, could ever become an object of beauty representing faith, hope, and love is an amazing miracle of transformation. Every cross adorning a church is in itself a sermon—a sermon proclaiming that if Christ can transform the Roman instrument of execution into a thing of beauty, there is hope that in Christ all things can be made beautiful! This is precisely the claim that the Christian faith makes concerning what Jesus accomplished in his death—and it is an astounding claim! The Christian claim is that through the execution of a particular Jew by a provincial governor in an eastern outpost of the Roman Empire during the first half of the first century, God was doing nothing less than saving the world! We should never lose sight of what an astonishing and even absurd claim this is. Nevertheless it is an absurd claim that Christian faith resolutely affirms. How God saves the world through the execution of Christ is a deep and many-faceted mystery, and one that does not give way to simplistic or formulaic explanation. But the church has always affirmed that the cross stands at the heart of our Christian faith, and we boldly confess that the cross is the locus of God's saving intervention as he acts within history. One way of viewing the cross through the lens of beauty is to see how at Golgotha the world was given a new axis—an axis of love.

What do I mean by an axis of love? An axis is a line around which an object or objects rotate—thus we speak of the earth rotating upon its axis. For my purposes, an axis can be understood as a centering principle that provides a funda-mental organization to a social structure. If we speak of our life having an axis, we are speaking of the essential meaning of our life, that which organizes our existence in a purposeful way. In using the image of an axis around which objects orbit, I am talking about identifying ultimate truth—that which is absolute and to which everything else is relative. In his cru-cifixion Jesus gave the world a new ultimate truth, a new axis around which to rotate—an axis of love. This is central to how God saves the world through the crucifixion of Jesus Christ. Let's explore what it means that the cross of Christ has given the world a new axis and some of the profound implications connected with it.

One of the most poignant aspects of Jesus's suffering must have been how alone he was in the knowledge of his impending crucifixion. Though Jesus had expressly told his disciples that his mission would inevitably lead to his crucifixion, this didn't seem to register with them. They simply could not accept it. In the minds of Jesus's disciples, a crucified messiah is a failed messiah. In their minds, the task of Messiah was to usher in the kingdom of God by overthrowing the kingdoms of the Gentiles. The coming of Messiah was anticipated as a violent overthrow of enemies in the mode of Joshua and David.

Jesus's followers were convinced that he was the Messiah and that he was going to succeed in bringing about the reign of God's kingdom—this is why they were following him. But they were utterly incapable of imagining how the kingdom of God could come *through* Jesus being crucified. Time and again Jesus's disciples made it clear that they did not believe Jesus was going to die. In their minds, Jesus's dying would mean failure, and they were convinced Jesus was going to succeed. Thus Jesus was left to face his impending death without the consolation of having a friend who understood what he was doing. Among the many sorrows of Christ is the distress of loneliness.

It's interesting to contrast how Jesus and Socrates approached their deaths. Both were just men sentenced to death by governing powers that did not understand them, but their attitudes toward death were quite different. Socrates, true to his Greek dualism, regarded death as liberation from the material world and thus went to his death cheerfully. But Jesus, as a Jew who believed the material world was God's good creation, approached death with an undeniable sense of dread. For Socrates, death was ultimately "no big deal." For Jesus it was. Jewish religious thought never had the afterlife orientation of the pagan Gentile religions. For the Gentile, death was an escape from the prison of this world. For the Jew, death was an affront to God's good creation. The Gentile hope was for an afterlife away from this world. The Jewish hope was for resurrection. For the Gentile, death could be reconciled as a friend. For the Jew, death was always an enemy. Yet Jesus understood that his mission would inevitably lead to his death. During his final week in Jerusalem Jesus expressed the anxiety he was feeling over his eminent death when he said, "Now my soul is troubled. And what should I say—'Father, save me from this hour'? No, it is for this reason that I have come to this hour."*

Part of the mission Jesus had received from his Father was to redeem all that it means to be human by entering into the full spectrum of human experience. Redemption of the human condition would come through Christ's full immersion into humanity in order to salvage it. This meant that as Jesus had entered the world by the universal human experience of birth, he would depart the world by the universal human experience of death. The Son of God would join humanity in the most human of experiences—birth and death. But his death would not be a peaceful fading away in old age; his would be a violent death in the prime of life. Jesus knew this.

From the beginning, Jesus knew that his life and message placed him on a collision course with the religious and political principalities and powers that would condemn him to death and execute him by crucifixion. In Jerusalem during his final week, Jesus spoke openly of his troubled soul. He then

---

* John 12:27

prayed, "Father, glorify your name." A voice from heaven said in reply, "I have glorified it, and I will glorify it again."* Or we could hear it like this: "Father, make your reputation beautiful." To which the voice from heaven replies, "I have made it beautiful, and I will make it more beautiful still." So we see that as Jesus contemplates his own impending death by crucifixion, his prayer is that it would somehow make the reputation of God beautiful. Jesus continued to unfold some of the mysterious purposes behind his imminent death when he said:

> "Now is the judgment of this world; now the ruler of this world will be driven out. And I, when I am lifted up from the earth, will draw all people to myself." He said this to indicate the kind of death he was to die.
> —JOHN 12:31–33

Jesus, in speaking of his anxious soul, announces that he is about to be "lifted up." "Lifted up" was a polite euphemism for crucifixion. In the first-century world, crucifixion was such an ugly spectacle that the word itself was often deemed inappropriate for use in polite company. What Jesus is doing in speaking of his being "lifted up" is making it clear that he understands how he is going to meet his violent death; it won't be by, say, secret assassination, but through a trial and a public execution by means of crucifixion at the hands of the Romans. Crucifixion was a means of execution administered only by the Roman government and only upon those they deemed a threat to their empire, especially revolutionaries and rebellious slaves.

Jesus is also saying some more mysterious things in this passage. First of all, Jesus indicates that somehow his death

---

* John 12:28

by crucifixion is going to drive out Satan from being what he calls "the ruler of this world." Jesus also says that his crucifixion in some way judges and condemns the world, intimating that the trial of Jesus in the court of Pilate was actually the trial of the world in the court of Christ. Finally Jesus says that as a result of being lifted up in crucifixion, he would draw all people to himself—in other words, by his crucifixion Jesus would give the world a new axis, a new organizing principle, a new order of arrangement, a new ultimate truth! How all of this comes about is one of the most beautiful and astonishing aspects of the gospel.

After Jesus was betrayed by Judas with a kiss in the Garden of Gethsemane, he was brought before the Jewish high priest Caiaphas and the ruling counsel of the Sanhedrin for a religious trial. There he was convicted of blasphemy for claiming to be the Messiah, the Son of God, and for asserting that he was the Son of Man—the mysterious figure spoken of by the prophet Daniel as the one who receives dominion over the Gentile nations from the Ancient of Days, thus establishing the global reign of the kingdom of God.* Jesus even told Caiaphas, "From now on you will see the Son of Man seated at the right hand of Power and coming on the clouds of heaven."† This was Jesus's explicit claim that he was establishing the kingdom of God and receiving a divine right to rule the nations. For this claim Jesus was condemned as a blasphemer.

Following his religious trial Jesus was brought before the Roman governor Pontius Pilate for a civil trial. When Caiaphas and the chief priests informed Pilate that Jesus had

---

* See Matthew 26:57–68; Daniel 7:9–14.
† Matthew 26:64

already been convicted of blasphemy, Pilate had no interest in the case and simply wanted to dismiss the matter. Pilate had no desire or motive for involving himself in the intricacies of Jewish religious controversy. In response, Caiaphas pursued a different tactic, a political one. Caiaphas pointed out that Jesus's messianic claim was not merely a religious matter but was primarily a political one. To claim to be the Jewish Messiah was a claim to be the Jewish king—it's what it meant to be the Messiah. If Jesus's claim to be the anointed Jewish king was religious blasphemy to the high priest Caiaphas, it was political insurrection to the Roman governor Pilate. The Jews already had a king—King Herod, the man appointed by Caesar to be the king of the Jews. If this Galilean was making a rival claim for the Jewish throne, it was a political matter. Thus Pilate was forced to investigate the case concerning Jesus of Nazareth and his seemingly ridiculous claim to be a king.

Jesus was brought into Pilate's headquarters for interrogation. Pilate asked Jesus the decisive question, "Are you the King of the Jews?"* Jesus gave a tacit acknowledgment and then said, "My kingdom is not from this world. If my kingdom were from this world, my followers would be fighting to keep me from being handed over to the Jews. But as it is, my kingdom is not from here."† We should make clear what Jesus was and was not saying. Jesus was not saying his kingdom was not *for* this world, as if it were merely a "spiritual" kingdom or a kingdom off in outer space somewhere; rather Jesus was saying that his kingdom was not *from* this world—it was not based upon the assumed world order. What Jesus was saying to Pilate can be understood as something like this: "Yes, I

---

* John 18:33
† John 18:36

am a king. But the reign of my kingdom in this world will not come about the same way that all the other kingdoms of this world have come about. The empires of the pharaohs and Caesars came through violent revolution and warring armies. My empire does not come in this manner; it does not come in the way of this world. But it comes."

At this point Pontius Pilate was understandably somewhat confused. How can a person really be a king if his kingdom does not come from this world? So Pilate restates his original question, asking, "So you are a king?" Jesus answered, "You say that I am a king. For this I was born, and for this I came into the world, to testify to the truth. Everyone who belongs to the truth listens to my voice." Pilate then gave his now famous and cynical reply—"What is truth?"*

Jesus was then taken away and flogged by Roman soldiers. After being flogged, Jesus was returned to Pilate's headquarters, this time bloody, crowned with thorns, and draped in purple as a mockery of his kingly claims. As Pilate resumed his questioning, Jesus now remained silent. In frustration Pilate said, "Do you not know that I have power . . . to crucify you?"† And there it is! In this moment the truth comes out— Pilate had answered his own question. "What is truth? I tell you what the truth is! The truth is—I have power to crucify you!" Power is truth. The power to kill is ultimate power and ultimate truth. This was Pilate's paradigm of truth. In the end it is the truth of power enforced by violence that is the ulti- mate truth of the principalities and powers. The truth of power enforced by violence is the axis around which the world ruled by the principalities and powers revolves. Power—especially

* See John 18:37–38.
† John 19:10

the power of violent force—is the ultimate truth, the bottom line, the organizing principle for those who are under the spell of Satan as the ruler of this fallen world.

Pontius Pilate told Jesus of Nazareth the "truth," hoping this dreamy Galilean would come to his senses and face reality—Pilate's reality. Pilate is in effect saying, "Look, you seem harmless enough, and I don't want to have to execute you, but you have to face reality; you have to accept the truth. The truth is that the world is run by people of power, people like Caesar, people like me. Just admit you're not a king, and you can go free. But if you continue to challenge our power by claiming to be a king, you will have to face the truth, and the truth is, I have power to crucify you." This is Pilate witnessing to Jesus and giving him the gospel of empire. (Interestingly, the term *gospel* was originally a Roman term for an imperial proclamation.)

What is truth? In their first encounter, Jesus had stated that he came into the world to bear witness to the truth. Now in their second encounter, Pilate bears witness to his truth. Both are "evangelizing" the other. This is a highly significant drama, and we must not fail to recognize what is going on here. In the meeting of Christ and Pilate, we find a collision of gospels and a contest for truth. For Pilate the gospel truth is that the world is run by men of power, and the ultimate power is the power to kill. As long as a person understands this truth and this gospel, he can organize his life accordingly. But this is not the truth and the gospel to which Jesus bears witness. Jesus came into the world to give it a new truth and a new gospel—the gospel truth that God is love!

Jesus and Pilate represent two different truths, two different gospels, two different axes, two different ways of organizing the world. From one perspective Christ is being tried in Pilate's imperial court. From another perspective (the Christian perspective) Pilate and the whole world are being tried in the court of Christ. Nietzsche, not surprisingly, thought that Pilate got the better of Jesus in their exchange and regarded it as the only genuine moment of nobility in the New Testament. Nietzsche essentially agreed with Pilate and considered power enforced by violence as the closest thing this world has to ultimate truth. For those under the spell of the ruler of this world, the Nietzschean truth of power enforced by violence is self-evident; it's simply the way the world is. You can resist it if you like, but in the end you will be crucified…and when you're dead, you're dead.

There is a deep irony in the way Pilate (and the empire he represented) viewed the cross. Pilate could have easily said, "The cross is truth." By which he would have meant, power is ultimate reality and ultimate power is the power to kill. Violence is reality. Violence is truth. The cross is truth. To which Jesus could have replied (and the Christian gospel does reply!), yes, the cross *is* truth. But the cross is not truth in the power to kill, but in the choice to love. *Ultimate truth is not power enforced through violence, but love expressed through forgiveness.* From the day that Cain killed Abel, ultimate reality seemed to be that the world was organized around the principle that those who possess the power of violence run the world. This has been the story of world history, and what a bloody history it has been. But Christ came to give a bloody world a new narrative, a new way of telling the human story. Instead of a world organized around power and violence, Christ came to give the world a new organizing principle, a new axis. Christ came to bring to the world a new government that would be organized around love and forgiveness. This is how the cross becomes an axis of love. Understanding the gospel of Christ as a new organizing principle and an axis of love is how the gospel is liberated from the shrunken world of private pietism and instead portrayed upon the large canvas of world history. It's the gospel writ large. But the gospel writ large has a lot of troubling implications concerning the way we tend to assume the world is arranged, which may explain why the gospel was relocated to the less threatening dimension of private piety in the first place.

It was into a brutally pragmatic world where ultimate truth was the power to crucify that Jesus was born. The pagan world was a world where the strong rule the weak, and the meek inherit the wind. But the birth of a child laid in a manger in Bethlehem would challenge this established order, and the principalities and powers knew it from the outset. The very birth of this child—a child the prophet Isaiah called the "Prince of Peace"—incited Herod to employ the ultimate truth of lethal violence. Why? Because a Prince of Peace threatens the axis around which the principalities and powers have organized the world—an organization that is decidedly to their advantage.

And so before this child could even talk, the despotic King Herod sent his death squads to Bethlehem...and Rachel weeps for her children, refusing to be comforted, because they are no more.* This is the dark side of Christmas. To maintain their axis, the principalities and powers will slaughter the innocents and even innocence itself. But this Prince of Peace, whom the principalities and powers instinctively recognized

---

*   Matthew 2:18

as a threat to their order and tried to murder while still a baby, survived Herod's slaughter and grew up to make the most astounding and subversive claim of all: *I am the truth.* In making the ultimate claim—the claim to be truth itself, Jesus was announcing that he was about to re-center the world. The world would no longer be centered around the truth of violence; it would now be centered around the truth of forgiving love—a truth to which he would bear witness all the way to the cross. Jesus was going to re-center the world around an axis of love!

The world desperately needed to be re-centered. It was off its axis. It was tearing itself apart. Humanity had lost its way— humanity had lost sight of God. Confusion reigned. The engines of war propelled human history, and history was being propelled into the outer darkness. The vision of God had been obscured by the fog of war and violence. The vision of God is always grossly distorted when viewed through the bloody lens of violent pragmatism and vehement nationalism. But this is what humanity had done as kings and priests harnessed God to its engines of war. Every tribe and nation claimed that God was their god, and their god was always some version of the Roman god Mars with his horrid trumpets of war. Under the demonic spell of violence, Satan had turned God's good world into a living hell. Even though we know it's true, when it matters most we almost always forget that "war is Hell. It is the outer darkness beyond the reach of love, where people who do not know one another kill one another and there is weeping and gnashing of teeth, where nothing is allowed to be real enough to be spared."[1] This was the world of Pharaoh's Egypt, Alexander's Greece, and Caesar's Rome. It was a world founded on violence and framed by war. It was a world where despite the fact that the noble virtues of family, loyalty, and justice could be found within the empire, the empire itself was founded upon the final truth of violence. Cain killed Abel, and violence became the axis around which the world revolved.

The world of the Roman Empire was held captive by the "pragmatic truth" of the principalities and powers. The *Pax Romana* was the established order. The great empire of Rome was able to bring "peace" to this world because any resistance at all to Roman authority was immediately crushed by the great military power Rome possessed. The gospel of the "Roman Peace" was "surrender to Caesar or we will kill you." Of course the rhetoric of propaganda would be employed to temper this "awful truth." This was the Roman Empire in the days of Caesar Augustus. But it was also the fullness of time. It was time for the Logos to become flesh, Truth to be made incarnate, and the invisible God to be revealed in human form. This was the only way for the truth of God to be liberated from the agenda of empire. The human vision of God had become distorted by the conscription of God into the service of war. But now humanity would finally see God *as he is*. "No one has ever seen God. It is God the only Son, who is close to the Father's heart, who has made him known."*

But the truth of God in human form would not receive a warm welcome from the powers that ruled the world. From the very beginning—from his heralded birth in Bethlehem, his first sermons of hope in Galilee, his proclamation of a new world order called the kingdom of God—the trajectory of Jesus's life placed him on a collision course with the "ultimate truth" of the Roman Empire. It was inevitable that the

---

* John 1:18

truth of Christ would collide with the truth of empire in the form of a Roman cross. Jesus knew this from the beginning of his ministry and had explicitly said so during his final weeks:

> See, we are going up to Jerusalem, and the Son of Man will be handed over to the chief priests and scribes, and they will condemn him to death; then they will hand him over to the Gentiles to be mocked and flogged and crucified; and on the third day he will be raised.
>
> —MATTHEW 20:18–19

During that final momentous week in Jerusalem, rival claims to ultimate truth were meeting face-to-face. The stage was set for a decisive confrontation. Christ was on trial in the court of Pilate. The world was on trial in the court of Christ. The principalities and powers were condemning Christ. Christ was condemning the principalities and powers. Pilate bore witness to the truth of power. Christ bore witness to the truth of love. It was an epic contest of truth claims. It was a collision of kingdoms—one from this world, one from heaven. The Prince of Peace stood before the representatives of political power and colluding religion wearing a crown of thorns. Pilate said, "Behold the man." From the crowd there arose the lusty chant of, "Crucify him! Crucify him!" Pilate taunted the chief priests for whom he had no respect: "Shall I crucify your king?" The chief priests didn't miss a beat: "We have no king but Caesar."* And there it is! Now all the cards were on the table. All the truth was out in the open. Pilate's truth was the power to crucify. Caiaphas's truth was the same as Pilate's— power enforced by violence. Ultimately the Roman governor

---

\* See John 19:1–15.

and the Jewish high priest served the same truth. Though they made a show of religion, the keepers of the temple also knew that the world revolved around the axis of violent power. This is supremely demonstrated when Caiaphas explicitly told the ruling council that the temple (as their center of power) had to be defended by a conspiracy to murder Jesus.*

Pilate's truth and Caiaphas's truth, despite outward appearances, were one and the same. There was no denying it. In the end, Pilate and Caiaphas shared the same truth. When Caiaphas and the chief priests confessed, "We have no king but Caesar," they showed their true colors. They also betrayed everything Moses and the prophets and the entire Hebrew tradition stood for! In that moment, the chief priests took off their religious masks to let Pilate know they knew how the real world is run. They were in on the secret. They knew the score. The power to kill is the ultimate truth. So they would pray their prayers and make a show of religion—for that was their charade—but in the end they would confess that their real king was the one who could command armies and unleash the greatest power with the most violence. No wonder a political insider like Pontius Pilate would cynically ask, "What is truth?"—and then walk away. He knew that "all the truth in the world adds up to one big lie."[2]

> So he delivered him over to them to be crucified.
> —JOHN 19:16, ESV

Pilate had issued his verdict. He had condemned Jesus of Nazareth to death by crucifixion because this naïve Galilean refused to face the only truth there was in the world—the

---

* See John 11:47–53.

truth of power enforced by violence. Yes, Jesus could hold onto his claim of being a king with a kingdom that was not from this world, but he would be crucified for it. To make his point, Pilate ordered the inscription to be placed on Jesus's cross: "Jesus of Nazareth, the King of the Jews."* It was the end of the line. The trials were over. The principalities and powers had handed down their verdicts. The religious powers had convicted Jesus of blasphemy. The political powers had convicted Jesus of insurrection. They had both sentenced Jesus to death. The death of the prophet from Galilee would not be an assassination in the dark, but a state-sponsored, religiously endorsed execution in broad daylight. Pilate's truth of capital punishment had trumped Jesus's truth of love and mercy.

> So they took Jesus; and carrying the cross by himself, he went out to what is called The Place of the Skull, which in Hebrew is called Golgotha. There they crucified him.
>
> —JOHN 19:16–18

Jesus had witnessed to the truth of love and the hope of the kingdom of God, and for it he was sentenced to death. What did Jesus do? He lived his sermon all the way to the end and loved relentlessly. He loved the world, a world that had rejected him. He loved his disciples, disciples who had forsaken him. He loved his enemies, enemies who had crucified him. And he forgave them all! Think about it—*he forgave them all!* From the cross Jesus spoke: "Father, forgive them; for they do not know what they are doing."† Then he died. The Apostles' Creed sums it up like this:

---

\* John 19:19
† Luke 23:34

[He] suffered under Pontius Pilate,
   was crucified, died, and was buried;
   he descended to the dead.

The End. Except it's not the end! It's not the end because
of the greatest surprise in history—a surprise that has become
the very cornerstone of Christian faith and confession. The
Creed continues:

On the third day he rose again;
   he ascended into heaven,
   he is seated at the right hand of the Father,
   and he will come again to judge the living and the
      dead.[3]

In the context of a courtroom drama where Jesus was tried
and convicted by Caiaphas and Pilate, do you see what the
resurrection means? The resurrection of Jesus Christ is much
more than just a happy ending; it's the Judge's surprising verdict! It was the verdict of heaven's Supreme Court, and it overturned all the verdicts of the rulers of the world. Caiaphas and
Pilate and the principalities and powers of this world had condemned and executed Christ for blasphemy and insurrection.
But the Father vindicated Jesus by raising him to life again!
The verdict of the resurrection affirmed that Jesus *is* the Christ
and he *is* Lord. The resurrection of Jesus Christ is the Father's
validation and vindication of his Son! Pilate had borne witness to the tired and cynical "truth" that the world is ordered
around the principle of power, and especially the power to
kill. Jesus had borne witness to a new and beautiful truth—
the truth of forgiving love expressed in forgiveness. The principalities and powers tried to convince humanity that all gods
are a kind of Mars and that violence is just the way the world

is run. Jesus said this was a lie, because God is love, and went to his death affirming his witness.

As long as Jesus lay dead in the grave, the principalities and powers could congratulate themselves on maintaining a world ordered around the axis of power and propose a toast "to the way things have always been." But on the third day the Father acted and issued his overturning verdict! He overturned the verdicts of Caiaphas and Pilate. He overturned the verdicts of political power and colluding religion. God vindicated his Son and validated the revolutionary truth Christ proclaimed. With the events of Good Friday and Easter Sunday the world was given a new axis—the axis of love.

This is beautiful! The greatest beauty of all! It really is the beauty that saves the world! It saves the world from the pernicious lie that power and violence have to be the foundation of human social order. In the crucifixion of Christ the principalities and powers are named and shamed, and their "truth" of violence is at last exposed for the ugly lie that it is. At the cross Jesus cast out Satan as the ruler of the world and gave the world not only a new ruler but also a new center, a new axis. In Christ the world no longer revolves around the pragmatic truth (lie!) of power enforced by violence. In Christ the world now is re-centered around the beautiful truth of love expressed in forgiveness.

Pilate was right; the cross *is* truth. But not the truth of pragmatic violence; rather the cross is the truth of co-suffering love. The cross of state-sponsored violence by which the rulers of the fallen world order retain their power became the means by which the world is liberated from their tyranny and reoriented around love. This was entirely unanticipated by the principalities and powers. The apostle Paul wrote about it when he said, "None of the rulers of this age understood this; for if they had, they would not have crucified the Lord of glory."* Remember, glory can be understood as beauty. Pilate didn't understand it. Caiaphas didn't understand it. Herod didn't understand it. Caesar didn't understand it. None of the principalities and powers understood it. What Jesus was doing was beyond anything they could understand or imagine. It was a radical new paradigm. Jesus was remaking the world based on a beautiful new idea. Jesus endured the cross and forgave his enemies. Jesus could have unleashed armies of avenging angels and kept the world centered around an axis of power. But he didn't. Instead he simply forgave his enemies and breathed his last. Why? So that the violent ways of the principalities and powers might be exposed and extinguished by the truth of unquenchable love. In this supreme demonstration of love, humanity came to know once and for all what God is really like!

> Being disguised under the disfigurement of an ugly crucifixion and death, the Christ upon the cross is paradoxically the clearest revelation of who God is.[4]
> —HANS URS VON BALTHASAR

Never again could the principalities and powers that enforce their will by violence claim God's endorsement. Never again! They had been exposed, and God had been revealed. God is beautiful. God is love. God is like Jesus. God has always been like Jesus. We have not always known this...but now we do. Jesus had said that if he was lifted up in crucifixion, he would draw all people to himself. The event of the crucifixion gave

---

* 1 Corinthians 2:8

the world a new ordering axis, a new ultimate truth, a new centering point—and it is love. The love of God was fully displayed in Christ at the cross when he forgave the world for its sins. If we want to know what God is like, we now point to Jesus on the cross forgiving a world that has rejected him, and we say, "There! That is what God is like!" And having now been vindicated in resurrection, Christ is drawing humanity into a new orbit, an orbit around himself and his redeeming love. All of this is beautiful. It is this beauty that saves the world.

The orbit around the axis of power is an orbit of chaos and hostility, fear and revenge. This is what we see in Homer's *The Iliad* and Machiavelli's *The Prince*. It is the hideous truth that is hidden in Machiavellian politics and exposed in Homeric war. In a world where ultimate truth is the power to kill, fear will be the motivating factor and pain will be the currency of payback. A life built around the axis of power will seek relief from pain by inflicting pain on others. This analysis helps us understand the dynamics of a wide spectrum of human conflict—from petty revenge to bloody ethnic feuds. The kinetic energy found in pain as payback guarantees that life will be as Thomas Hobbes described it in *Leviathan*:

> ...where all mankind [is in] a perpetual and restless desire of power...[in] continual fear, and danger of violent death; and the life of man [is] solitary, poor, nasty, brutish, and short.[5]

Thomas Hobbes, the seventeenth-century English political philosopher, presented his solution for a violent and dangerous world ordered around the axis of power—where "the life of man [is] solitary, poor, nasty, brutish, and short"—in the creation of an all-powerful state: The Leviathan. Hobbes's theory was that people would enter into a social contract with an all-powerful state in order to keep some semblance of security and civility. But that Thomas Hobbes named his book on social contract theory *Leviathan* is an obvious admission that he merely hopes to tame the beast of empire—because like Pilate before him and Nietzsche after him, Hobbes believed that the world has no choice but to be ordered around the axis of power. Yet this is precisely what Jesus Christ and the cross as an axis of love saves the world from! This is what the kingdom of God provides an alternative to! The Lamb of God saves us from Hobbes's leviathan! There is a better choice than having to choose between different versions of monsters— Revelation's beast or Hobbes' leviathan—there is the kingdom of the Lamb built around the axis of love!

But to come into Christ's orbit around the axis of love we must believe in Jesus. *Really* believe in Jesus! Yes, believe the orthodox doctrines of his virgin birth, his divine identity, and his bodily resurrection. But also believe *the gospel he proclaimed*—a gospel of the kingdom of God where the ordering principle and central axis is co-suffering love and radical forgiveness. In this alternate ordering of human society we don't seek relief from our pain by inflicting it on our enemies, but instead we are healed by the wounds inflicted on Christ. Our violent ways find an end in the wounds of Christ, and in his forgiveness we are offered healing from our self-inflicted pain.*

Jesus is not just saving individuals and leaving the world as it has always been—dominated by principalities and powers under Satan's spell. No! Upon the cross Jesus is re-creating the world! The orbit of pain around the axis of power becomes

---

\* See 1 Peter 2:21–25.

transformed into the orbit of peace around the axis of love. The orbit around the axis of power is inevitably an orbit of chaos, hostility, and revenge. But the orbit around the axis of love is an orbit of grace, forgiveness, and peace. If we can learn to look at Christ upon the cross and see it, not as tragic, but as beautiful, we can be drawn into his new and life-giving orbit. By looking to Christ on the cross, Satan is exposed as a liar and murderer and forsaken as an enemy of humanity.

It is through the cycle of revenge that Satan remains the ruler of the world. But as people look at Christ upon the cross and see him giving the world a new axis, Satan as the ruler of the world is driven out. Satan is not cast out in some "magical" way because Jesus was crucified; rather Satan is cast out because Jesus gave the world a new axis—a world ordered around the axis of love becomes a world in which Satan has no place! When we look to Christ upon the cross and see it as the supreme demonstration of divine love and allow ourselves to be drawn into a new orbit around this axis of love, Satan simply has no place—he is driven out.

> Now is the judgment of this world; now the ruler of this world will be driven out. And I, when I am lifted up, will draw all people to myself.... The light is with you for a little longer. Walk while you have the light, so that the darkness may not overtake you. If you walk in the darkness, you do not know where you are going. While you have the light, believe in the light, so that you may become children of light.
>
> —Jesus, in John 12:31–32, 35–36

> I am writing you a new commandment that is true in him and in you, because the darkness is passing away and the true light is already shining. Whoever

says, "I am in the light," while hating a brother or sister, is still in the darkness. Whoever loves a brother or sister lives in the light, and is such a person there is no cause for stumbling. But whoever hates another believer is in the darkness, walks in the darkness, and does not know the way to go, because the darkness has brought on blindness.

—THE APOSTLE JOHN, IN 1 JOHN 2:8–11

John's commentary on what Jesus said about becoming children of light makes it clear that if we haven't come into an orbit around the axis of love, we are still in the dark, orbiting around the dead star of a black hole called *hatred*. And who is the one we hate? The one we refuse to recognize as a brother, the one upon whom we refuse to confer the dignity of shared humanity. We dehumanize our enemy so we can demonize our enemy and hate them with imagined impunity. But it's nothing more than orbiting around the black hole of hatred, a black hole that in the end will consume all its satellites. A social structure where core identity is based upon a shared hostility is a social structure where Satan is still the ruler of the world.

Where the axis of power maintains the orbit of ancient hostilities through envy and bitterness there is, as the apostle James described, "disorder and wickedness of every kind."* It is what we have seen in the Middle East between Israelis and Palestinians, in the Balkans between the Serbs and Croats, in Rwanda between the Hutus and Tutsis, in Northern Ireland between Catholics and Protestants. It is from this kind of unending hostility and violence that Jesus saves the world by giving the world a new axis. The point the apostle John is

---

* James 3:16

making in his epistle is that a salvation that doesn't bring us into the axis of love is no salvation at all. Until we come into a new orbit around the axis of love, we are still in the dark.

Christ upon the cross giving the world a new axis is the beauty that saves the world—from its sin, from its intractable hostilities, and from the dominion of the principalities and powers. The apostle Paul is always effusive in his praise of what the cross has accomplished. In his letter to the Colossians, Paul tells us that the principalities and powers were shamed and publicly humiliated by the cross.* To understand how the cross shames the principalities and powers is to understand how Jesus has re-centered the world around a new organizing principle. But first we must ask: "What exactly is meant by 'principalities and powers' (or rulers and authorities)?" Principalities and powers are the power structures within society—political, economic, religious, and so forth. These are the institutions that shape our world. But it must be recognized that enormous centers of power tend to take on a spirit of their own, and it's usually not good. As Lord Acton famously observed, "Power tends to corrupt and absolute power corrupts absolutely."[6]

When the power structures within a society allow expediency to compromise ethics, they become corrupt and demonic. When this happens, it can bring tremendous harm to vast numbers of people, perhaps millions. The lust for domination inevitably brings institutions under the influence of the god of this world—the false god who rules from an axis of power. This is how Satan rules the world. History bears witness to the immense amount of human suffering that is

---

* See Colossians 2:15.

directly attributable to powerful institutions driven by self-centered ambition. Governmental institutions can become oppressive and brutal. Economic institutions can become corrupt and exploitative. Religious institutions can become manipulative and abusive. These realities dominate our news headlines—another military dictatorship...another political abuse of power...another exposé of corruption on Wall Street...another corporation exploiting child labor...another sexual abuse scandal in the church. When the institutions of power make their bid for more and more power, lots of people get hurt.

In the passion drama of Christ the principalities of political, economic, and religious power were on full display. Pontius Pilate as the Roman governor represented the *political power* of the Roman Empire. Herod Antipas represented *economic power*. (The Herodian family was one of the wealthiest families in the first century, amassing a fortune surpassing even that of the Roman emperors.) The high priest, Joseph Bar Caiaphas, clearly represented *religious power* in collusion with political and economic power. These three men were the representative figureheads of the principalities and powers responsible for the crucifixion of Christ. Pilate, Herod, and Caiaphas perceived in Jesus of Nazareth a threat to the existing arrangement, a challenge to the status quo of a world organized around an axis of political, economic, and religious power. So they set themselves against this Galilean who claimed to be the Son of God and King of the Jews. As the psalmist said:

> Why do the nations conspire,
>   and the peoples plot in vain?
> The kings of the earth set themselves,

and the rulers take counsel together,
against the Lord and his anointed.

—PSALM 2:1–2

The principalities and powers opposed the one who claimed to be the anointed Messiah—*by murdering him!*—because they had a correct instinct that Israel's Messiah posed a real threat to the way the world had always been arranged. Jesus himself had said that in the kingdom he was bringing, "many who are first will be last, and the last will be first."* So all three of these men, representing the principalities and powers of the present age, conspired in the execution of Jesus of Nazareth because he posed a threat to "the system."

Yet the gospel message is that Jesus triumphed over the principalities and powers. Paul says it like this: "He disarmed the rulers and authorities and put them to open shame, by triumphing over them in it."† What is going on here? How does death on a cross triumph over the established principalities and powers?

First we need to understand that the word *triumph* does not technically refer to victory in a battle but to the victory parade following the battle. In Rome, the generals of vanquished enemies would be paraded naked through the main thoroughfares of the city and thus subjected to public shame and humiliation. Shame and humiliation were also part of the psychological torture of crucifixion—which is why victims were always crucified naked. Even though artistic depictions of the crucifixion of Christ add a bit of clothing for modesty's sake, Jesus was crucified naked. It was part of the shameful nature of

---

* Matthew 19:30
† Colossians 2:15, ESV, margin

crucifixion. Yet Paul says that in some way the cross was a shaming of the principalities and powers. In some way the crucifixion of Christ was the public humiliation of the rulers and authorities in the manner of a Roman triumph. But how does this work? How does the shameful humiliation of Christ upon the cross result in the shameful humiliation of the principalities and powers?

It works like this: The principalities and powers always claim they are good and just and that God is on their side. It is an essential aspect of their propaganda. More likely than not, they believe their own propaganda. A good propagandist must first excel at self-deception. Even if the world is arranged around an axis of power where the ultimate power is power to kill, this truth is rarely made explicit. Instead, the propaganda "talking points" are dutifully adhered to: "We are doing what is good. We are bringing justice to the world. God is on our side." Certainly Pilate, Herod, and Caiaphas made these kinds of claims, and to a certain extent they probably believed them. But the cross refutes their propagandistic claim of being good and just. The cross humiliates the principalities and powers by exposing their naked grasp for power.

Watch how this works: The principalities and powers justify their positions of power by asserting they are good and just and that God is on their side. But when the Righteous One, the Just One, the very Son of God came among them, what did they do? They murdered him! In the crucifixion of Jesus, it was not Jesus who was put to shame, but the principalities and powers. Pilate and Herod and Caiaphas all claimed a commitment to goodness, justice, and God's will. But the cross exposes the emptiness of their claims. They did not possess goodness, justice, or God's endorsement—they only possessed the will to power. In the light of the cross, self-centered power brokers are stripped naked and put to public shame.

But how do we *know* that Jesus was the Just One and not Pilate, Herod, and Caiaphas? How do we *know* that Jesus was the Righteous One and not the principalities and powers? Is it simply that we have a preferential inclination toward Jesus's version of morality and justice? Is it merely a matter of taste, as Nietzsche might suggest? (Admittedly I prefer Jesus's sense of the beautiful over Nietzsche's, but it's more than that.) We know that Jesus was the Just One because... *God raised him from the dead!* This is why the resurrection is the cornerstone of Christian faith. It changes everything. Seen through the lens of the resurrection, the cross is no longer the shameful public humiliation of Christ, but the shameful public humiliation of the principalities and powers! In the light of the death and resurrection of Christ, principalities and powers arranged around an axis of power can no longer claim to be good and just—their claim has been invalidated by the cross.

Now as people look upon the cross, having believed in the validation given to Christ by God in the resurrection, they see its beauty and begin to be drawn away from the axis of power—they are drawn into a new orbit around an axis of love. As this happens, the world is given a new order, a new order in which there is simply no longer any room for Satan. Satan stays in business as the ruler of the world by manipulating people through fear, greed, the desire to dominate, and the impulse for retaliation. He whispers in our ears insidious suggestions like: "You're not getting your fair share. You need more. They hurt you, and you need to hurt them back." A world under that kind of arrangement will be impelled by fear and full of hatred, violence, and war. Peace will simply be a breathing spell between rounds of conflict.

But as we are drawn into a new orbit, a new world arranged around the cross of Christ, we respond to the satanic whispers with words like these: "I'm losing my false life for the sake of the gospel that I might find my real life. It's the meek who will inherit the earth. Yes, I know they hurt me, but I forgive them." In such a world, Satan simply has no place. As Jesus himself said, "The ruler of this world is coming, and he has nothing in Me."* This is the peace of Christ. When our lives are reordered around the cross as an axis of love, the enticements of Satan, which are so persuasive within the axis of power, simply fail to resonate with us. We are set free from the demonic tyranny that unleashes hell. In the new world order arranged around an axis of love, the government of Messiah's peace begins to take hold.

The apostle Paul makes further claims concerning the undoing of the principalities and powers in his letter to the Ephesians when he says that it is God's intention "that through the church the wisdom of God in its rich variety might now be made known to the rulers and authorities in the heavenly places."† The principalities and powers not only claim to be good and just, but they also claim to be wise. The principalities and powers claim to be "the smartest men in the room." They are the "brightest and best" whose right it is to rule the world. These are the ones who are best qualified to shape society. But this too is shown to be a lie. The principalities and powers *don't* know how to run society; what they know how to do is employ their genius in the maintenance

---

* John 14:30, NKJV
† Ephesians 3:10

of an axis of power—an arrangement that is suited to their advantage. The Roman agenda was first and foremost to keep Rome rich and powerful.

The great promise of every empire is peace and security. But it's a promise no empire can ever really deliver. Paul says it like this: "When they say, 'There is peace and security,' then sudden destruction will come upon them."* Wendell Berry puts it this way, "Ceaseless preparation for war is not peace."[7] The true task of the rulers and authorities is to deliver peace, to produce a just, peaceable, and livable society. This is the kind of peace that the prophets called *justice* and Jesus called *abundant life*. But though peace is always the promise of the principalities and powers, it's a promise they are incapable of delivering. In a world arranged around an axis of power, peace will always remain elusive. A peace achieved by violence is at best a temporary cessation of hostilities. In a world arranged around an axis of power, the enemies of peace are constantly energized.

The achievement of a community of peace is how the church demonstrates the wisdom of God to the principalities and powers. What the ruling principalities cannot produce in their world arranged around an axis of power enforced by violence, the church centered around an axis of love is to actually produce. This is accomplished as people are drawn from the entire spectrum of society—from the whole range of ethnic, social, economic, and political distinction—and formed into a new unified humanity called the *body of Christ*. As this happens, the church, as God's new humanity in Christ, demonstrates the wisdom of God to a world bereft of peace in its

---

* 1 Thessalonians 5:3

arrangement around an axis of power. The creation of a peaceable people is proof of God's wisdom! Paul says it like this in describing how Jews and Gentiles are brought together in the peaceable kingdom of Christ:

> But now in Christ Jesus you who once were far off have been brought near by the blood of Christ. For he is our *peace*; in his flesh he has made both groups into one and has broken down the dividing wall, that is, the hostility between us. He has abolished the law with its commandments and ordinances, that he might create in himself one new humanity in place of the two, thus making *peace*, and might reconcile both groups to God in one body through the cross, thus putting to death that hostility through it. So he came and proclaimed *peace* to you who were far off and *peace* to those who were near.
>
> —EPHESIANS 2:13–17, EMPHASIS ADDED

When the church actually lives as the peaceable kingdom of Christ, it is a demonstration of the wisdom of God to the principalities and powers. Furthermore, it's the ultimate demonstration that Jesus is Lord and Caesar is not! Caesar cannot produce real peace, but Christ can! This is why peace and unity within the body of Christ must be regarded as absolutely sacred. If we are not a peaceable people, we impugn the credibility of the gospel of peace. The God of peace who crushes Satan under the feet of the saints does not do so through the means of human violence, for that would be collaboration with ways of Satan.* Violence cannot defeat Satan; it only energizes the monster. The God of peace crushes Satan under the beautiful feet of his peaceable servants as they follow the ways of the

---

* See Romans 16:20.

Lamb. God's vision for society is not some version of Caesar's kingdom—to which Pilate and Herod and Caiaphas all swear allegiance—but the alternative society of the kingdom of God arranged around the cross as an axis of love.

Jesus was not trying to give the world the best version of Caesar's kingdom; he was giving the world the kingdom of God! And this kingdom is distinguished for its capacity to produce peace. This is why Jesus refused to be drawn into any of the many heated political controversies of his day. Political controversies were simply irrelevant to what Jesus was doing in giving the world a radical new alternative. Through the new humanity of the body of Christ, "we are made members of a kingdom governed by a politics of forgiveness and redemption whereby the world is offered an alternative unimaginable by our sin-determined fantasies."[8] The "kingdom governed by a politics of forgiveness and redemption" is the new world built around the cross of Christ as an axis of love and a world where Satan is driven out. It is the only real possibility for peace. It is the beauty that will save the world.

The only institution that can claim the title of "Christian"  is one that is actually Christlike. For an institution to claim to be Christian, it must take up the cross and follow Jesus in the most demanding of Christ's ethical imperatives—loving and forgiving enemies. The principalities and powers of this world simply cannot do that. They belong to a structure organized around an axis of power; their entire orientation is one of retaliation, and their only paradigm is vengeance. Only the church empowered by the Spirit and organized around an axis of love can forgive enemies. It is only in obedience to Christ's radical imperative of enemy-love that the church has a right to lay claim to the noble moniker of *Christian*. Christ sends forth his church as sheep among wolves.* This is why martyrdom is always a possibility for the Christian. Quite simply, we are disciples of the one who would rather die than kill his enemies. This is why the second-century church father Tertullian said, "The blood of the martyrs is the seed of the church."[9] We will not kill for our faith, but we will die for it. Theologian David Bentley Hart says:

> Christianity can only return to its understanding of peace, its unique style of rhetoric, as the sole source of accord; it must always obey the form of Christ, its persuasion must always assume the shape of the gift he is, it must practice its rhetoric under the only aspect it may wear if it is indeed Christian at all: martyrdom.[10]

Hart's insistence that we "always obey the form of Christ" and "always assume the shape of the gift he is" returns us to the idea of beauty. Beauty always has form. Adherence to the beautiful form is what makes a thing beautiful. The beautiful form of Christianity is the cruciform. The most radical shape of the cruciform is martyrdom. The killing of enemies is the form of redemptive violence within a world arranged around an axis of power. Martyrdom is the form of redemptive violence within a world arranged around an axis of love.

On October 8, 2010, Dritan Prroj, a thirty-four-year-old pastor in Shkoder, Albania, was murdered as he was on his way to pick up his two young children from school. He was shot six times, three times in the head. Dritan Prroj was murdered because his family was involved in a blood feud that began five years earlier.[11] Blood feuds have been a part of Albanian society for centuries, especially in northern Albania.

---

* Matthew 10:16

According to the "law" of the blood feud, if someone is killed, then the family of the victim has the right (or even an obligation!) to avenge the death by killing another male from the other family. These blood feuds wear on until all the males of one family are dead. This is an extreme example of a culture arranged around an axis of power enforced by violence. It is an ugly evil generating a debilitating effect upon the culture. It is the rule of Satan. People who have lived and ministered in Albania tell of hundreds of men living in hiding in northern Albania for fear of deadly reprisal in the unending cycle of violence. Families and villages are paralyzed in this poor region, as the men of entire extended families don't dare to venture outside their homes.

Dritan Prroj lived for a considerable time as a "captive" in his own home, but eventually decided he could not succumb to the evil of blood feuds and would choose to live openly. He and his brother determined that if one of them was killed, the other would not "take blood" in an exercise of revenge. They would simply allow the cycle of violence to die with them in a deliberate imitation of Christ. Dritan Prroj had remarked to others that he felt his life might be used to help bring an end to this terrible plague. In the year leading up to his death, Dritan and his church helped lead a large program to aid flood victims in their region, as well as other social justice programs. As a result, Pastor Prroj was well known in his community and highly respected as a man of peace. When he was murdered, there was extensive coverage of his death in newspapers, magazines, and television. His death helped expose the false "honor" behind the demonic philosophy of blood feuds. Two weeks after his death, a large rally was held in the capital city of Tirana with thousands of people turning out to name and shame the senseless destructiveness of ceaseless and senseless blood feuds. Many carried signs that read, "To forgive is manly"—a concept completely contrary to cultural assumptions and one that undermined the insidious foundation of the blood feuds. A friend who has lived and ministered in the Balkans sent me an e-mail the day of the rally in Tirana; in it he said:

> It is beautiful to see the church stand up against the cultural lies in their society and present an alternative of hope. Dritan once told a friend of mine that he felt his life might help bring an end to the blood feuds in Albania. His allowing the evil to be shown for what it truly is, is shaming the principalities and powers and revealing a more beautiful way. I thought you might enjoy hearing about Dritan Prroj and his courage to live a life of beauty, which would cost him everything, a life which at first glance makes it look like evil has won but on second glance helps undo the very evil that took his life.[12]

This is the church showing the wisdom of God to the principalities and powers. This is a demonstration of how a satanic power structure of violence and revenge that has dominated a culture for centuries is being named and shamed through a church inspired by a pastor who chose to be a martyr instead of an avenger simply because it is the Jesus way. It is the story of a faithful Christian who, in his death, is helping recover beauty for a culture that has lost its way in the ugliness of violence and revenge. This is the cruciform in its most radical form. It is in the axis of love expressed in forgiveness that the axis of power enforced by violence is exposed as ugly. It is in the axis of love expressed in forgiveness that Satan is cast out. It is in the axis of love expressed in forgiveness that Jesus reigns as the Prince of Peace. It is in the axis of love expressed in forgiveness that we find the beauty that will save the world.

*Two stories have haunted us and followed us from our beginning.... We carry them along with us like invisible tails—the story of original sin and the story of Cain and Abel. And I don't understand either of them. I don't understand them at all but I feel them.*[1]

—Samuel Hamilton in *East of Eden*

## CHAPTER 4

# EAST OF EDEN

W E LIVE IN a world gone wrong. It's been going wrong for a long, long time. This is an important part of the story the Bible tells. The story of humanity as told in Scripture begins with a man named Mankind (Adam) and a woman named Life-Giver (Eve). Mankind and Life-Giver transgressed God's command by eating from a forbidden tree called the knowledge of good and evil. Mankind and Life-Giver ate of the knowledge tree to become like God, and in a sense they did. God said, "See, man has become like one of us, knowing good and evil."* The problem is that mankind is no good at being like God apart from God. Being able to choose between good and evil and being able to choose wisely are two different things. From the dawn of human civilization, the sons of Adam and daughters of Eve have exercised their capacity to choose good and evil, right and wrong for themselves. But the witness of history is that

---

* Genesis 3:22

these choices are consistently poor, misguided, self-centered, and lead to disastrous consequences. Thus human history is a bloody tale. This is the story the Bible tells.

But the Bible also tells the story of God's efforts to save a world gone wrong. It is a long and complicated story with many twists and turns and with plenty of apparent failures and dead-ends, but the story eventually leads to Jesus. And as the Christian story is told, it makes this enormous claim: Jesus came to save the world. It's a claim that sounds common in our ears coming after two thousand years of Christian history, but it tends to be understood in a very narrow and constricted sense. Too often the salvation brought to the world by Jesus is presented as almost exclusively pertaining to our "spiritual condition" and the afterlife—a salvation that is private and postmortem.

The Bible does not present Jesus as only the savior of human individuals (though he is that too) but also as the savior of human society. Human society—by which we mean people living together in some form of community—is God's design and part of God's good creation. To be human is to be necessarily social. We are created to bear the image of God and to care for one another—to worship God and be our brother's keeper. We become fully human only in a social context. Language, art, and culture are social achievements. Since human society is part of God's good creation, it is something God intends to save. Salvation is not just *me* "getting saved" (though it includes that). Salvation is both personal and social. Salvation is God saving what he has lost. Salvation is the Lord's salvation, and the Lord's salvation is not an evacuation project but a restoration project.

In the centuries since the birth of the modern era, the

obsession with the private self has tended to obscure the larger canvas of human society that God is working upon. We can't see the forest for the trees. We can't see the world for the individual. Since the Enlightenment, modern Christians have taken to reading the Bible in a highly individualistic manner, which is largely a misreading. Nearly every time you read "you" in Paul's epistles, it is in the plural. We also tend to think of the world as merely a collection of individuals, but this too is a mistake. The world is not just an aggregate of individuals; it is also civilization and human society as a whole, and God intends to save it. Thus Jesus is the savior of souls (individuals) *and* the savior of the world. This is why the apostle John wrests the imperial title of "Savior of the World" away from Caesar and daringly bestows it upon Jesus.* From the apostolic point of view, Jesus does not just save human individuals; he also saves God's intention for human society. Why is God so interested in human society? For the simple reason the apostle John famously records: "For God so loved the world."†

To understand how human individuals have gone wrong, we look at the story of Adam and Eve and their attempt to be like God apart from God. To understand how human civilization has gone wrong, we look to another Genesis story—the story of Cain and Abel. This is the story of two brothers, their enmity, and the first murder. It is the tragic story that moves the human saga east of Eden.

Cain and Abel—the first brothers, our ancestors. Cain was a tiller of the ground. Abel was a keeper of flocks. Cain was a farmer. Abel was a shepherd. The vocations of the brothers are an important clue to understanding the story. Anthropologists

---

\*  John 4:42; 1 John 4:14
†  John 3:16

tell us that human civilization developed as humans learned how to harness the power of agriculture. As human society progressed from hunter-gatherer communities to agricultural communities, they were enabled to settle in one place and were thus given the opportunity to develop more complex civilizations and more sophisticated cultures. But land would also be viewed differently within an agricultural community. Land would now be property—property that could be owned and thus fought over. We know historically that enmity would often arise between settled agriculture communities and nomadic shepherd communities. Farmers didn't want shepherds grazing their flocks in their fields. The Bible records the deep animosity that the agriculture-based empire of Egypt held toward the nomadic shepherd communities of Canaan.* This drama of conflict is played out in microcosm in the story of Cain and Abel. Eventually the conflict between Cain and Abel reaches a crucial point. Genesis tells the story in a single verse:

> Cain said to his brother Abel, "Let us go out into the field." And when they were in the field, Cain rose up against his brother Abel, and killed him.
>
> —GENESIS 4:8

There is something in the sparse way the story is told that makes this episode all the more sad. Cain gives his brother an invitation to join him in the field. Abel obliges and seems oblivious to any malicious intent. Abel comes to Cain for what he perhaps imagines to be an outing of brotherly camaraderie. It turns into a murder. We wonder if Abel ever saw

---

* See Genesis 46:33–34.

it coming. Alone in the field and away from prying eyes Cain thinks he has gotten away with it. But he didn't get away with it. God comes to Cain and pointedly asks, "Where is your brother Abel?" Cain says, "I don't know. Am I my brother's keeper?" As if to say, "How should I know? Am I supposed to keep track and take care of my brother like he keeps track and takes care of those sheep of his?" (I hope by now we at least know the correct answer to the question.) Then in one of the most poignant passages in the Bible we read God's reply and the sad events that unfold as a result of Cain's murder of his brother:

> And the Lord said, "What have you done? Listen; your brother's blood is crying out to me from the ground! And now you are cursed from the ground, which has opened its mouth to receive your brother's blood from your hand. When you till the ground, it will no longer yield to you its strength; you will be a fugitive and wanderer on the earth." Cain said to the Lord, "My punishment is greater than I can bear! Today you have driven me away from the soil, and I shall be hidden from your face; I shall be a fugitive and a wanderer on the earth, and anyone who meets me may kill me." Then the Lord said to him, "Not so! Whoever kills Cain will suffer a sevenfold vengeance." And the Lord put a mark on Cain, so that no one who came upon him would kill him. Then Cain went away from the presence of the Lord, and settled in the land of Nod, east of Eden.
>
> —GENESIS 4:10–16

So much pathos and so much importance is found in this Genesis passage. It is with a forlorn sadness that God asks Cain, "What have you done?"—a question he already knows the answer to. God knows Abel has been slain because he hears. "Listen! Your brother's blood is crying out from the ground." Of course Cain didn't have ears to hear the cry of his slain brother's shed blood, but God always hears. (Just as he would later hear the cry of the Hebrew slaves suffering in the empire of Egypt.) So as the blood of Abel cries for justice, a curse comes upon Cain. He will now wander the earth an exiled man bearing a mark that will unleash sevenfold vengeance. As Cain departs from the presence of the Lord he is headed east of Eden, and it won't be long before Eden is long gone.

Human society has moved far east of Eden, but we still retain in memory the promise of paradise...and how we long to get back to the garden! But is it possible? We know a lot, we have amassed information, we possess sophisticated technology, but we don't know how to find our way back to Eden. We've wandered so far east...

In the Book of Genesis, to move east is symbolic of moving away from God, away from good, and toward evil and destruction. When Adam and Eve were driven out of Eden, they departed to the east.* When Cain went away from the presence of the Lord, he went east.† It was as human society migrated eastward onto the plain of Shinar that they built the tower of Babel in their rebellion against God.‡ When Lot separated from Abraham, he settled to the east in the doomed city of Sodom. So the expression "east of Eden" is a word picture of humanity moving away from God and headed for trouble. In the Genesis story, as Cain moves east of Eden into

---

* Genesis 3:24
† Genesis 4:16
‡ Genesis 11:2

the land of Nod, we are told he builds a city.* The city that Cain builds is the first city in the Bible—it's the Bible's depiction of the emergence of human civilization. Cain lays the foundation for human civilization, and we, all of us, live in the city that Cain built—but Cain is a murderer. Indeed this is the disturbing truth: human civilization is founded around an axis of power established by murder and enforced by violence. The dark specter behind the history of human civilization is that it is almost always founded on acts of violence. We hide this dark specter behind façades of glory and patriotism, but the specter remains and from time to time the ghost comes out to haunt us.

As Genesis continues to tell the human story, we find that five generations after Cain, humanity is picking up speed as it flies away from Eden. Listen to what Cain's descendant Lamech tells his wives:

> Adah and Zillah, hear my voice;
>   you wives of Lamech, listen to what I say:
> I have killed a man for wounding me,
>   a young man for striking me.
> If Cain's revenge is sevenfold,
>   then Lamech's is seventy-sevenfold.
>
> —GENESIS 4:23–24, ESV

Cain's sevenfold vengeance has now become a seventy-sevenfold vengeance as violence gains a demonic kinetic energy and pushes human civilization to the brink of self-destruction. The generation following Lamech brings about the ominous "days of Noah," described in Genesis like this:

---

\* Genesis 4:17

> Now the earth was corrupted in God's sight, and the
> earth was filled with *violence*. And God saw that the
> earth was corrupt; for all flesh had corrupted its ways
> upon the earth. And God said to Noah, "I have deter-
> mined to make an end of all flesh, for the earth is
> filled with *violence* because of them; now I am going
> to destroy them along with the earth."
>
> —GENESIS 6:11–13, EMPHASIS ADDED

In the days of Noah, human civilization was corrupting
itself (literally *destroying* or *ruining* itself). How? By violence.
It's interesting that the only sin specifically mentioned as producing the moral ruin of civilization in the days of Noah is
violence. We tend to luridly imagine other sins of moral decadence, and no doubt they were present, but still the only sin
mentioned is the sin of violence. The lesson we are to learn
from the story of Noah is that human civilization founded on
murder, obsessed with vengeance, and saturated with violence
is doomed to destruction. I've often thought how Christian
interest in expeditions to find Noah's ark instead of engaging
in efforts to rid the earth of violence really is an exercise in
missing the point!

I question whether contemporary Christians share the same
attitude toward violence as presented in Genesis. I tend to
think we do not. How often have we said or heard something
like this: "Yes, the movie is rated R, but only for violence."
That's what we say—"only for violence." The implication is the
movie is compatible with Christian values as long as there is
no sex in it, "only violence." But "only violence" is what led to
the destruction of human civilization in the days of Noah! So
why do we give violence a free pass? I have my suspicions, and
they are dark suspicions indeed. We overlook violence because

it is the very foundation of the city Cain built east of Eden. We fear that to take a stand against violence would undermine the very foundation of our civilization. This is our fear, so we cling to our violence.

Western civilization is largely the heir of the great Roman civilization. The Roman Republic and Empire of antiquity, the Holy Roman Empire of the Middle Ages, the European nation-states of the Renaissance, the liberal democracies of modernity in Europe and North America lead to what we understand as Western civilization. This is what makes the founding myth of Rome so significant for us and worth looking at. And how did the ancient Romans tell the story of the origin of their great civilization? Like the biblical story of Cain and Abel, the Romans had their own story of brothers, the twins Romulus and Remus.

As the story is told, Romulus and Remus are fathered by the war god Mars, but they are left to die by exposure in the wild. Fortuitously the twins are found by a she-wolf that suckles and raises them. Once grown, the brothers set out to found a great city. But there arises a dispute between them concerning its location. Romulus wants to found the city on Palatine Hill, while Remus prefers Aventine Hill. As the dispute grows violent, Romulus murders his brother Remus. With his brother now slain, Romulus is free to found his city on Palatine Hill (the site of Caesars's imperial palace), and he names the city for himself—Rome. Romulus then creates the Roman legions to wage the wars and the Roman Senate to govern the state. Thus, according to the myth, Roman civilization was founded by Romulus who murdered his brother Remus. A kind of pagan version of Cain and Abel. Other civilizations have similar founding myths.

J. R. R. Tolkien created a parallel myth in his epic *The Lord of the Rings*. The humanlike Sméagol murders his brother Déagol on Sméagol's birthday to gain possession of the ring of power, which Déagol has found. Over time the ring of power corrupts Sméagol into the devious and reptilian Gollum—an apt metaphor of Lord Acton's axiom about the corrupting nature of power. (Remember how Gollum mutters tenderly over the ring of power, calling it his "precious.") And that is the story of human history, whether it's told as Cain and Abel, Romulus and Remus, or Sméagol and Déagol—we want our "precious," we want the ring of power, and we are willing to kill our brothers to get it. It's the foundation of human civilization. Whether it's Babylon, Rome, or Mordor, we live in cities founded on a bloody lust for power.

But we tend to shrug our shoulders at it all. We tell ourselves it's just the way it is. It's the way the world is run. It's why we fight our wars. We do it to preserve our "precious"— our freedom, our rights, our race, our nation, our power, our position, our superiority, our economy. We overlay all of this with the trappings of glory. And there is a glory and beauty in it—the glory of heroic sacrifice for hearth and home that we commemorate in statues, memorials, poems, and anthems. But it is a glory and beauty that for all its heroism is too often a façade to hide the bodies of Abel, Remus, and Déagol—our slain brothers.

Now we turn our consideration to the most important person in Genesis, and really the most important person in the Old Testament—Abraham—the man whose life marks a turning point in humanity's flight from Eden. What was Abraham looking for as he left the great and cultured civilization of Ur and journeyed . . . *west?* The direction of Abraham's journey is significant. After all those Genesis journeys east-ward, someone is now headed west. But what was Abraham looking for? Why would Abraham leave an advanced civiliza-tion with all the amenities of a sophisticated city to become a wandering nomad living in tents? Abraham was looking for something, something God had called Abraham to search for. The Bible tells us Abraham was looking for a *city*. But not just any city; Ur was a city after all. Ur was a large, advanced, cul-turally sophisticated city. Despite the advantages of living in Ur, Abraham was looking for a different kind of city. Or let's say it this way: Abraham was looking for a new way of orga-nizing human society, a new type of civilization. The writer of Hebrews tells the story this way:

> By faith Abraham obeyed when he was called to set
> out for a place that he was to receive as an inheritance;
> and he set out, not knowing where he was going. By
> faith he stayed for a time in the land he had been
> promised, as in a foreign land, living in tents, as did
> Isaac and Jacob, who were heirs with him of the same
> promise. For he looked forward to the city that has
> foundations, whose architect and builder is God.
> —HEBREWS 11:8–10

It's important to understand what Abraham was looking for. Abraham was looking for a civilization that was according to God's design—a city whose architect and builder is God. Abraham was looking for something other than the archi-tectural design given to the world by Cain and his heirs. Abraham was looking for a way of building a city where the cornerstone would not be laid with the shed blood of a slain brother. Abraham wasn't just looking for a new place to pitch his tent; he was looking for a new way of structuring human society! Abraham wasn't merely trying to escape the mean city and find peace and quiet in the country. Abraham was looking for nothing less than a new social order. He was looking for some "other" way. Could there be an alternative to the system of civilization as power enforced by violence?

Abraham was looking for a city that, instead of killing Abel, Remus, and Déagol, made room for them. Abraham was looking for a city that was not east of Eden. Abraham was looking for a Jerusalem—the city of shalom. A peaceable city is what Abraham was looking for! This is why he journeyed west. If we can keep the Bible's big story in mind, we can see that what God was doing through Abraham would ultimately lead to that new city, but it would be a very long and complex process. And it would happen in a way no once could have predicted. During his lifetime Abraham would not find the city of peace he sought for, but he would see it from afar. This is what the writer of Hebrews means when he says:

> All these died in faith without having received the promises, but from a distance they saw and greeted them. They confessed that they were strangers and foreigners on the earth, for people who speak in this way make it clear that they are seeking a homeland. If they had been thinking of the land that they had left behind, they would have had opportunity to return. But as it is, they desire a better country, that is, a heavenly one. Therefore God is not ashamed to be called their God; indeed, he has prepared a city for them.
>
> —Hebrews 11:13–16

It's all too easy for us to mishear what the writer of Hebrews is saying concerning the quest of Abraham and the patriarchs. Abraham was not looking for a city *in* heaven; he was looking for a city *from* heaven. Abraham was looking *on earth* for something that would come *from heaven*. Abraham was looking for God's city to come, for God's will to be done on earth as it is in heaven. If Abraham had merely been looking to go to heaven, there would have been no need to leave Ur, journey west, live in a promised land, receive a son by faith in his old age, establish a covenant people, and all of that. If Abraham's goal had simply been to go to heaven, he needed only to stay in Ur and die. Simple. But that's not what Abraham was looking for. He was looking for a city on earth built by God and not by Cain.

Neither was Abraham looking for some improved version of Cain's city. Abraham wasn't looking for Ur with a Better Business Bureau. If that had been the case, Abraham could have simply returned to his old city or never have left in the first place. No, Abraham had to leave Ur because he was simply not at home there; he was not comfortable with the way the world was run. Abraham was looking for something else, a better country, a heavenly city, a more beautiful way of structuring human society. Abraham had to leave Ur because God had called him to look for (and help to found) something better. This is why Abraham journeys west.

It's interesting how even in our own culture and vernacular a westward journey evokes the notion of looking for something new. "Go west, young man!" Because Abraham was looking for something radically new and not merely improved, God said, "Go west, old man!" Likewise to "go back east" is an idiom for giving up on an idealistic vision. The American pioneer who couldn't take the rigors of western expansion would pull up stakes and "go back east." The writer of Hebrews commends the faith of Abraham, Isaac, and Jacob because, despite hardships, they did not give up and "go back east." Therefore God was not ashamed to be called the God of Abraham, Isaac, and Jacob. And God would not leave them disappointed, for he had prepared a city for them.

> Yet all these, though they were commended for their faith, did not receive what was promised, since God had provided something better so that they would not, apart from us, be made perfect.
>
> —HEBREWS 11:39–40

The heroes of the eleventh chapter of Hebrews all made their contributions to the legacy of faith, but none of them received the ultimate promise—the city of God. Abraham, Isaac, and Jacob become wandering sojourners living in a land of promise. Moses delivered a nation out of slavery, gave the Hebrew nation a new law, and led them to the borders of a new homeland. David became a king, made Jerusalem his capital city, and established a royal line of succession to sit upon his throne. All of these patriarchs, prophets, and kings had their role to play in the purposes of God, but the city of God was still not built. It would not be built and could not be built until the Cornerstone came, until the Cornerstone was laid. The promise of the city of God was inseparably linked with the hope for Messiah. Abraham would not receive this city in his lifetime, but he would see it from afar, as Jesus said to his critics in Jerusalem: "Your ancestor Abraham rejoiced that he would see my day; he saw it and was glad."*

---

* John 8:56

Therefore, since we are surrounded by so great a cloud of witnesses, let us also lay aside every weight and the sin that clings so closely, and let us run with perseverance the race that is set before us, looking to Jesus the pioneer and perfecter of our faith, who for the sake of the joy that was set before him endured the cross, disregarding its shame, and has taken his seat at the right hand of the throne of God.

—HEBREWS 12:1–2

The great men and women of faith depicted by the writer of Hebrews all bear witness to the validity of a life lived by faith in God. These were the pioneers of faith who "went out west" in search of the city of God. They all had their adventures of faith, and in their lives they proved the faithfulness of God. Their exploits of faith are renowned. It is in this way that they are a "great cloud of witnesses"—they testify to the possibility of the faith life. But the ultimate prize, the great promise, the grand object of their quest was the city of God, and this was not found. At best they saw glimpses of it. But what they all did with their lives of faith was to point us to the one who would come to build the city of God—Jesus! When Jesus came, he was not only a pioneer of faith like those who had gone before him, but he was also the perfecter (or "goal") of faith. What the men and women of faith had longed for and looked for is fulfilled in Jesus. What Jesus accomplished is what set Abraham on his journey in the first place. Jesus would be the founder of the city of God. The better city Abraham was looking for, Jesus would build! The just nation Moses was looking for, Jesus would found! The righteous kingdom David was looking for, Jesus would establish! The peaceable city Solomon was looking for, Jesus would construct! If in the ancient world all roads led to Rome, in the Bible all faith journeys lead to Jesus. For those who long for a better way to be human and look for a better way to structure human society, Jesus is the searcher's end.

Abraham, Moses, Joshua, David, Solomon, and many others all played their part in building Jerusalem—the city of peace. And at its best Jerusalem was, from time to time, a hopeful glimpse of what could be. But for the most part Jerusalem was no different from any other city, at least in terms of producing peace and justice. Before its first destruction in the sixth century B.C., the prophets denounced Jerusalem as a "bloody city,"* and a generation before its second destruction in the first century A.D. Jesus said the guilt of "all the righteous blood shed on earth, from the blood of Abel to the blood of Zechariah"† would come upon Jerusalem. So despite its promising name of "City of Shalom," Jerusalem was just another city of Cain built on the shed blood of slain brothers. What was needed was a *new* Jerusalem! A *real* city of peace!

That Jesus is the founder of the new city of God, the New Jerusalem, the true city of peace, is one of the great overarching themes of Scripture. But unlike Cain and Romulus, Jesus founds his city, not by killing, but by dying! Instead of mounting an army to overthrow his enemies in bloody war after the manner of all great civilizations, Jesus instead mounts the cross, forgives his enemies, and simply dies. Jesus refuses to found his city in the manner of Cain and Romulus; Jesus instead founds his city in the manner of Abel and Remus! Jesus does not shed the blood of others to found his city; he

---

* Ezekiel 22:2; see also Ezekiel 25 and Nahum 3.
† Matthew 23:35

shed his own blood! This is so counterintuitive! This is unheard of! This is absurd! This is scandalous! And this is the gospel!

But still the incongruence is jarring. How can Abel and Remus found a city? They were the brothers who were slain! Precisely. This is the mystery and offense of the gospel. It challenges our most basic assumptions of how the world is run and how civilization is structured. Since the death and resurrection of Christ, Cain and Romulus can no longer be lionized as heroes who rise to greatness by virtue of their superior strength. Instead they are shamed by the triumphant Christ who, instead of slaughtering his rivals, becomes the slaughtered lamb. It's a parody that makes a mockery of all of our most cherished myths and legends. And if we find this gospel disturbing, then perhaps we are on our way to rediscovering a gospel that is once again newsworthy!

The writer of Hebrews reminds us how Jesus endured the cross and disregarded the inherent shame of crucifixion. Jesus was able to disregard the shame of crucifixion because, as we saw in the previous chapter, it was not Jesus who was shamed as he was stripped naked and nailed to the tree—instead, it was the principalities and powers who were stripped naked and shamed. The cross strips the principalities and powers of their pretense and exposes the shame of their naked ruthlessness. We now know that the cross displays the glory and beauty of Christ, while at the same time it exposes the shame and nakedness of the principalities and powers. We know all of this by virtue of Christ's resurrection as God's vindication of his Son. Furthermore, Christ is not only risen; he has also ascended to the right hand of God and now rules the nations as the world's true Caesar. The seminal Christian confession of "Jesus is Lord" carries with it the implicit claim that Caesar is not! The new empire of the Lord Jesus Christ was the gospel the apostle Paul was so intent on proclaiming in the imperial capital of Rome and before Caesar himself. No wonder they cut off his head!

What are we to make of all this? Can it be true? Has Jesus really founded the city Abraham was looking for so long ago? Is Jesus really the anti-Cain who founds his city in the manner of Abel? How real is this city? Is it a city we can actually live in here and now? The writer of Hebrews is very bold in his answer:

> But you have come to Mount Zion and to the city of the living God, the heavenly Jerusalem, and to innumerable angels in festal gathering, and to the assembly of the firstborn who are enrolled in heaven, and to God the judge of all, and to the spirits of the righteous made perfect, and to Jesus, the mediator of a new covenant, and to the sprinkled blood that speaks a better word than the blood of Abel.
>
> —HEBREWS 12:22–24

In this one, long, marvelous, bold sentence, the writer of Hebrews takes the reader all the way back to the origins of human civilization—the shedding of the blood of Abel—and he says, "Now everything has changed!" *Now* we have come to Mount Zion! *Now* we have come to the city of God! *Now* we have come to the heavenly Jerusalem! *Now* we have at last found the city Abraham was looking for! *Now* there is a new way of structuring human civilization! Jesus has built a new city! New in what way? Cain's city was built on the shed blood of a slain brother, and it became the pattern for all human civilization. But now Jesus has laid the foundation for a new city—a new way of structuring human civilization.

The cornerstone for Jesus's new city will not be dedicated with the shed blood of a slain brother. Instead Jesus will dedicate the cornerstone of the city of God with his own blood. Cain spilled the blood of his brother Abel, and that blood cried out against Cain. It cried for vengeance and brought a curse upon Cain and a curse upon all who would build their cities by killing their rivals.

But the blood of Jesus speaks a better word than the blood of Abel. Instead of crying out for vengeance, the blood of Jesus cries, "Father, forgive them!" Instead of the curse of shameful guilt, ever-escalating vengeance, and continual violence, the blood of Jesus brings the blessing of forgiveness, reconciliation, and peace. The blood of Jesus is the triumph of love. Instead of a civilization based on power enforced by violence, the world is given the possibility of a civilization based on love expressed as forgiveness. It is a peaceable kingdom that is given to the world in Christ the King. This is the glory and beauty of the gospel! "Beauty belongs continuously to the Christian story... and... it appears there as the gift of peace."[2]

Babylon and Rome, to be sure, have a veneer of glory and a semblance of beauty, but they always seem to hide the ugly truth that they have built their city on the shed blood of their brothers. The blood of Abel and Remus cry out in the consciences of Cain and Romulus. The cities of Babylon and Rome and all their heirs are built on murder. They are built on fratricide—brother killing brother. But the city of God is not built by a murderer; it is built by a martyr—a martyr who was resurrected as Lord and Savior. Jesus is a beautiful Savior who has nothing ugly to hide. The city of God is not built on the shed blood of slain brothers; it is a city founded on the shed blood of the one who forgave his enemies! The cross of Christ gives humanity a way to recover the lost beauty of Eden. The cross confronts the hidden ugliness of a civilization founded on fratricide and gives us a way back to the beauty of brotherhood.

> It is in the mystery of the crucified God that the deeply tragic nature of human existence is revealed to itself: if God has made death his own, paying the price of freedom to the last penny, here on this earth the way of the cross will always remain the way to freedom and beauty. Precisely because the eternal Son has drained the bitter cup to the lees, this way will always be the way to life, where beauty will be finally made known, never again to be hidden.... What we await at the end of the long Good Friday that is the history of the world is the victory and glory of beauty.[3]
>
> —BRUNO FORTE

Bruno Forte says the cross is the way to freedom and beauty, and, of course, he is right. This is what Jesus said over and over as he called his disciples to take up their own crosses and follow his example of radical enemy-love. But we have a hard time hearing this. It goes against everything we have been taught as we have grown up in Cain's city. Cain and Romulus and all those who found their cities by killing their brothers (whom they call enemies) always speak much of "freedom." But it's freedom as propaganda. Freedom is to them the *raison d'être* that justifies every action. Freedom is a popular slogan but a tricky concept. Freedom, like beauty, truth, and other abstract ideas, is one of those words that we can easily use but cannot easily define. So we twist it to suit our needs.

In the self-centered, serpent-influenced worldview of Cain and Romulus, freedom simply means power—no more, no less.

The world built upon Cain's version of freedom is the world as Nietzsche described it in *Beyond Good and Evil*—"simply Will to Power, and nothing else."[4] For Nietzsche, love was an illusion, and what makes the world go round is only the will to power. In this worldview, <u>freedom is inextricably connected with domination</u>. Freedom for Cain and Romulus is the power to do as they please and to employ violence against any who would impinge upon what they call their "freedom." For them, freedom is the will to power—the ability to dominate. The power to shape the world after their own liking. This kind of freedom demands the killing of enemies. Plain and simple. So if Abel and Remus stand in the way of Cain and Romulus doing or having what they want—their "freedom"—Abel and Remus will have to be slain. Cain's freedom is killing. Cain's freedom is domination. Cain's freedom is Nietzsche's will to power. (But at some point we who confess Christ have to decide if we are going to be Nietzschean or Christian!)

In the city of Cain, all things are permissible when done in the name of freedom. Freedom for Cain, Romulus, and Sméagol is ultimately the ring of power. But we have to ask ourselves: Having obtained the ring of power by killing our brother, how free are we? How free was Sméagol as he slowly turned into the grotesque creature Gollum? Gollum, distinguished only by treachery and violence, was anything but free. Gollum was quite obviously enslaved to the ring of power. It had robbed him of true freedom—the freedom to love. Sméagol transformed into Gollum was the antithesis of freedom. Gollum wasn't free—Gollum was a slave! That tells us something very important: <u>if freedom is nothing more than a euphemism for power, we can quite literally become slaves to our freedom!</u> This is one of the lessons we should learn from

*The Lord of the Rings* (if we haven't already learned it from the Bible!). In Tolkien's story, the ring of power was created by the Dark Lord Sauron for one purpose: to enslave the world. Thus the malevolent nature of the ring is revealed in the sinister inscription it bore:

> One Ring to rule them all,
> One Ring to find them,
> One Ring to bring them all
> And in the darkness bind them.[5]
> —J. R. R. TOLKIEN, *THE FELLOWSHIP OF THE RING*

 If freedom is nothing more than the impulse to "rule them all," it is nothing more than the will to power. This kind of freedom is the path to slavery and bondage. Freedom misunderstood as power is the tool of Satan to enslave the world to murder and violence. This is what Jesus was saying in his famous dialogue on freedom with the Judeans recorded in the eighth chapter of John's Gospel.\* Every major civilization and nation makes a claim that they are exceptional and free. It is the stock and trade of nationalistic propaganda. If any nation could ever have made a legitimate claim to such exceptionalism and freedom, it would have been Israel as the children of Abraham who were delivered by Moses out of their bondage in Egypt. But Jesus dismisses all of it. He flatly tells them they not free, but slaves of sin. Not only slaves of sin, but also children of Satan! Jesus said the proof that Satan is their father is evidenced by the murder in their hearts. They were trying to

---

\* See John 8:31–59.

kill him—as Cain killed Abel. Their response was to call Jesus a bastard* and then try to kill him!†

Obviously these people were very angry—angry enough to want to stone Jesus. That's what happens when you challenge people's concept of freedom—they lash out. Yet the fact remains that when we build our cities east of Eden on the shed blood of our slain brothers, we are never free, no matter how vociferously we insist we are. Jesus redefined freedom by associating it, not with power, but with love. The one who is free to love is truly free. But we don't want to hear this. We want to believe we are free if we simply have enough power to do what we want and kill those who get in our way. This is the kind of self-deception Jesus exposes. Jesus not only told the Judeans they were children of the devil, but he also told them they had listened to lies and deceived themselves. The lie they told themselves was that they were free. They had deceived themselves into thinking freedom is the power to impose your will on those around you. But it's all a lie. This is the kind of self-deception Dave Matthews satirizes in his scathing song "Don't Drink the Water." To kill others to make room for ourselves is one version of "freedom"—but don't drink the water!

It is this kind of murderous freedom—freedom as the ring of power that leads to the slavery of sin—that Jesus came to save humanity from. Jesus saves the world from false freedom, from freedom as a euphemism for power, from freedom as a justification for killing. It is in the same dialogue with the Judeans on freedom that Jesus exposes a nationalistic understanding of "freedom" as nothing more than collusion with Satan. Then Jesus speaks of Abraham seeing the new day that

---

\*　John 8:41
†　John 8:59

Messiah would bring and rejoicing in this true freedom. Of course not everyone wants to hear this. The response Jesus received for his redefinition of freedom began with insult and ended with an attempted stoning. Saving people from the false freedom of will to power in order to bring them into the true freedom of love can be a thankless task (to say the least!). But once you see it, once you are saved from the false freedom of will to power and find the true freedom of sacrificial love, the thanksgiving becomes eternal! It becomes the song of the redeemed.

They sing a new song:

"You are worthy to take the scroll and to open its
    seals,
for you were slaughtered and by your blood you
    ransomed for God
saints from every tribe and language and people and
    nation;
you have made them to be a kingdom and priests
    serving our God,
and they shall reign on earth."

Then I looked, and I heard many angels surrounding the throne and the living creatures and the elders; they numbered myriads of myriads and thousands of thousands, singing with full voice, "Worthy is the Lamb that was slaughtered to receive power and wealth and wisdom and might and honor and glory and blessing!" Then I heard every creature in heaven and on earth and under the earth and in the sea, and all that is in them, singing, "To the one seated on the throne and to the Lamb be blessing and honor and glory and might forever and ever!"

—REVELATION 5:9–13

The Book of Revelation is the only possible conclusion to the story the Bible tells, *if* the story is to be beautiful. John's vision as the apocalyptic finale of Scripture gives the Bible the beauty of symmetry and resolution. The garden lost in Genesis becomes the garden recovered in Revelation. Babylon as the ultimate city of Cain is finally overcome by the New Jerusalem as the promised city of the Lamb. The monstrous beasts that come up from the earth, from the sea, and from the pit are comically defeated by a little lamb—a slaughtered lamb that lives again! The wicked are outside the city and are not permitted to enter so as to disrupt the peace of the longed-for New Jerusalem. But those outside the city are invited to repent, wash their robes, and enter the city by the gates—for its gates will never be shut and the Spirit and the bride say, "Come!"* This is the mission of the church: to call humanity to forsake the burned-out and violent cities of Cain, come by faith and repentance, and at last enter the peaceable city of the Lamb. Yes, the Spirit and the bride say, "Come!"

But all of this is much more than just getting back to Eden or recovering the lost garden. In fact, it's not going back at all—it's moving forward into the eternal plans and purposes of God. To build the peaceable city is what was intended by God all along. The redeemed in Revelation proclaim before the throne of the Lamb, "Salvation belongs to our God who is seated on the throne, and to the Lamb!"† Which is to say, it is the *Lord's* salvation, for it is *God* who has suffered loss in the ruin of human civilization. In a world where Cain keeps killing Abel, it's not only Abel who suffers loss; God himself suffers loss. But God intends to recover what he has lost. God

---

\* See Revelation 21; 22.

† Revelation 7:10

has a salvation by which he will recover his peaceable vision for human society.

The problem wasn't that Cain founded a city. Civilization itself isn't the problem. The hope of Scripture is not a return to a "primitive innocence" of wearing loincloths and living on berries. Cities and civilizations were always God's good intention. The problem wasn't that Cain founded a city; the problem was that Cain founded his city on power enforced by violence where the dedicatory sacrifice was his brother's blood. Cain's murder of Abel placed the world on a course that would enable us through our advanced technology to eventually kill our brothers a million at a time with death camps, chemical weapons, and nuclear bombs. This is a world under the dominion of the dragon, the beast, and the false prophet, and hell-bent on Armageddon.* The Lamb saves the world from all of that. The Lamb gives us a way out of our demon-inspired, self-destructive, hate-fueled madness. The Lamb gives the world an alternative to endless Armageddons. The Lamb gives the world a new axis and new possibility for human civilization—love expressed as forgiveness where the dedicatory sacrifice is the blood of the Lamb. This is the beauty of the Apocalypse.

John the Revelator tells us that it is by the blood of the Lamb that we overcome the satan (the accuser). Think of it this way: it is by the blood of Jesus's co-suffering sacrifice of forgiving love that we overcome the accuser who instills enmity and murder between brothers and makes the world a bloody hell where Cain keeps killing Abel.† In the apocalyptic vision, the Lamb conquers the beast. This is the astounding

---

\* See Revelation 16:13–16.

† Revelation 12:10–11

hope of Revelation—the Christian hope that there is a better way than the way of endless Armageddons and Cain killing Abel a million at a time. The Lamb conquers all of that, and those who follow the Lamb are the called, chosen, and faithful.* In other words, we who confess Jesus as the Christ are called and chosen to be faithful in following the way of the Lamb.

This is the chief vocation of the church—to faithfully replicate the way of the Lamb and to resist paganism in all its forms. Are we doing this? Are we a faithful witness against the lies of paganism? We've heaped scorn upon Aphrodite, and we at least acknowledge Mammon is a lie, but sadly we're still prone to serve as a chaplain to Mars. But to be faithful we must learn the peaceable ways of the Lamb, for if the end is to be peace, then the means used must also be peaceful. "The means are the ends in the process of becoming."[6]

From as far back as Genesis a city was always intended. A civilization was always in mind. But not a city at the expense of the garden. Not a civilization that lays waste to the earth. Not a city that kills its brothers. Not a city east of Eden. What was intended was a city and civilization that *keeps its brothers* and *keeps the garden!* And that's exactly the vision John saw—the vision of a garden city of brotherly love. John saw a towering, gleaming city with enormous gates and broad thoroughfares, but with a garden in the heart of it. It's a city with rivers and mountains and trees and fruit—it is a garden city.† The nations walk in the light of this city; kings come to this city, not to make war, but to bring their glory.‡ It's Eden expanded into a

---

*    Revelation 17:14
†    See Revelation 21:9–22:5.
‡    Revelation 21:24

city—the city of God. The prophecy of John the Revelator is not just a prediction for a distant future, but an inspiration for our imagination as we seek to be those who live in the city of God here and now. For as the writer of Hebrews says to the saints, "You *have* come to Mount Zion and to the city of the living God, the heavenly Jerusalem."* But to live as citizens of the New Jerusalem here and now, we must be those who overcome the devil by the blood of the Lamb and don't cling to our own lives even in the face of death.† Christian de Chergé was one of these saints who lived as a citizen of the city of God here and now.

Christian de Chergé was a French Catholic monk and the Trappist prior of the Tibhirine Monastery in Algeria. With the rise of radical Islam in 1993, Father de Chergé knew that his life was in danger. But instead of leaving Algeria, Father de Chergé chose to stay and continue his witness to the gospel of Jesus Christ. On May 24, 1996, Father de Chergé was beheaded by Muslim radicals. Anticipating his death, Father de Chergé had left a testament with his family to be read upon the event of his murder. The testament in part read:

> If it should happen one day—and it could be today—
> that I become a victim of the terrorism which now
> seems ready to encompass all the foreigners living in
> Algeria, I would like my community, my Church, my
> family, to remember that my life was given to God
> and to this country. I ask them to accept that the One
> Master of all life was not a stranger to this brutal
> departure. I ask them to pray for me: for how could
> I be found worthy of such an offering? I ask them to
> be able to associate such a death with the many other

---

* Hebrews 12:22, emphasis added
† Revelation 12:11

deaths that were just as violent, but forgotten through indifference and anonymity.

My life has no more value than any other. Nor any less value. In any case, it has not the innocence of childhood. I have lived long enough to know that I share in the evil which seems, alas, to prevail in the world, even in that which would strike me blindly. I should like, when the time comes, to have a clear space which would allow me to beg forgiveness of God and of all my fellow human beings, and at the same time to forgive with all my heart the one who would strike me down....

Obviously, my death will justify the opinion of all those who dismissed me as naïve or idealistic: "Let him tell us what he thinks now." But such people should know that my death will satisfy my most burning curiosity. At last, I will be able—if God pleases—to see the children of Islam as He sees them, illuminated in the glory of Christ, sharing in the gift of God's Passion and of the Spirit, whose secret joy will always be to bring forth our common humanity amidst our differences.

I give thanks to God for this life, completely mine yet completely theirs, too, to God, who wanted it for joy against, and in spite of, all odds. In this Thank You—which says everything about my life—I include you, my friends past and present, and those friends who will be here at the side of my mother and father, of my sisters and brothers—thank you a thousandfold.

And to you, too, my friend of the last moment, who will not know what you are doing. Yes, for you, too I wish this thank-you, this "Adieu," whose image is in you also, that we may meet in heaven, like happy thieves, if it pleases God, our common Father. Amen![7]

—FATHER CHRISTIAN DE CHERGÉ

Christian de Chergé lived as a citizen of the city of God. The manner in which he died and the testament he left behind is the only Christian response to militant Islam I can think of that is faithful to the Lamb of God. Father de Chergé does not call for his blood to be avenged, but like his Savior, Father de Chergé prays for the forgiveness of his murderer and speaks of him as "my friend of the last moment, who will not know what you are doing." In his martyr's testament, Father de Chergé bids his murderer "Adieu" and hopes that they might meet in heaven "like happy thieves." This is beautiful. Father de Chergé overcame Satan by the blood of the Lamb and the word of his testimony, because he would rather die than follow the way of Cain. Commenting on the martyr of the Tibhirine Monastery, Stanley Hauerwas says:

> Christian de Chergé is a martyr made possible by Christ's death. His life is a witness that allows us to glimpse what it means to be drawn into the life of God, the Father, Son, and Holy Spirit, the life nailed to the cross. To so be made part of God's love strips us of all our presumed certainties, making possible lives like that of Christian de Chergé, that is, lives lived in the confidence that Jesus, the only Son of God, alone has the right to ask the Father to forgive people like us who would kill rather than face death. That is why we are rightly drawn to the cross, why we rightly remember Jesus' words, in the hope that we might be for the world the forgiveness made ours through the cross of Christ.[8]

The foundations of the city of God have been laid—Christ Jesus himself is the cornerstone. The city of Abraham's quest has been founded. The New Jerusalem, though obviously not fully present, is a city under construction. We live in the tension of the now and not yet. We cannot claim that the kingdom of God has fully arrived, but we dare not say the kingdom has not yet come. We live in the overlap of ages.

As a result of this reality the struggle between the city of Cain and the city of God continues. Babylon still seeks to silence the witness that comes from the New Jerusalem. It was Rome in the first century that resisted the witness of the lordship of Christ. In our own day it will be other empires, other institutions, other power structures that will resist our witness. Because of this we must accept that from time to time persecution may be our lot and that martyrdom remains a possibility. We may be called upon to bear the ultimate witness of the way of the Lamb to the children of Cain who are still building their violent cities east of Eden.

As followers of the Lamb, we are witnesses to the viability of a society structured in love over and against the violence of a society structured in power. N. T. Wright observes, "Power corrupts and the church should bear witness to that corruption by critique, by non-collaboration, by witness, and, if need be, by martyrdom."[9] But we do so as those who have departed from the land of Nod east of Eden and have found their way to the beautiful city Abraham so eagerly sought.

> We're marching to Zion,
> Beautiful, beautiful Zion;
> We're marching upward to Zion,
> The beautiful city of God.[10]

## CHAPTER 5

# I AM FROM THE FUTURE

THERE ARE THREE Josephs of note in the Bible. All three were men of exceptional character. They are: Joseph the son of Jacob who was sold into slavery and became the ruler of Egypt and whose life can be interpreted as a foreshadowing of Christ; Joseph the carpenter and husband of Mary who acted as a father to Jesus and taught Jesus his carpenter trade; and Joseph of Arimathea, the member of the Sanhedrin who took the body of Jesus down from the cross and buried him in his own tomb. Joseph of Arimathea is certainly the lesser known of the three, but I find him fascinating. As an act of love and devotion, he obtained permission from Pilate to give Jesus a respectful burial—something ordinarily denied to the victims of crucifixion. He took the body of Jesus from the cross and helped carry it to his nearby garden for burial in his own tomb. Think about it: a Jewish religious leader handling the corpse of a condemned criminal who had been hung on a tree...on the eve of Passover! All of this is remarkable and took a lot of courage. Luke tells us Joseph was a good and righteous man, and that even though he was a member of the ruling council that condemned Jesus to death, he did not consent to their plan and action.*

 Luke also tells us that Joseph was "waiting expectantly for the kingdom of God."† What does this mean? What exactly was Joseph waiting for? Joseph was longing for the God of Israel to intervene in history and at last set up his own government. Joseph had little faith in the corrupt regime of Herod, and he certainly had no faith in the pagan Roman Empire. If the government of God was going to come, it would have to come from outside of the current centers of power. What Joseph longed to see was what the prophets had promised: that God would act within history and set up his own government and bring about the reign of righteousness, justice, and peace—in short, the kingdom of God. Joseph knew God's reign was not going to come through the Herodian dynasty or the Roman Empire—he was hoping it would come through the young prophet from Galilee. This is what Joseph was waiting for.

Perhaps you relate to the longing that was in the heart of Joseph of Arimathea. Perhaps you too have lost confidence in the governments of this age to bring about righteousness, justice, and peace. Perhaps you too ache for the world to be set right and for the government of God to at last break in among men. If you share this holy yearning, I want to say something bold, daring, and decidedly radical, but absolutely true...

I am from the future.

I mean it. I am from the future. I know it sounds like a put-on, but I'm completely serious. It sounds like science

---

\* Luke 23:50–53
† Luke 23:51

fiction, but it's theological fact. It's not a childish fantasy; it's a spiritual reality. I am from the future. I am from the future because I've been born again. Let me explain.

Jesus told Nicodemus (a friend of Joseph of Arimathea and fellow council member who helped with the burial of Jesus) that in order to see the kingdom of God, he would have to be born again or, literally, be born from above.* Think of it like this: In order to perceive the kingdom of God that was coming into the world through what Jesus was doing, Nicodemus, the pre-eminent teacher within the conservative Pharisee movement, would have to take the radical step of rethinking everything he had ever assumed about how the kingdom of God would come and what it would look like. Nicodemus would have to be born from above or "take it from the top" and rethink his most cherished assumptions. Why? Because the kingdom of God was going to come in a different way and be far different than Nicodemus had imagined. Unless Nicodemus was willing to do this—to rethink everything—he would not be able to see the kingdom of God, even though it was right in front of him. The problem was that Nicodemus was held captive to the assumptions of the Pharisees. The Pharisees assumed that Messiah would be one of their own and that he would act in the manner of Joshua, David, and Judah Maccabaeus and lead a conventional revolution against their Roman occupiers in order to set up the kingdom of God. But they had it all wrong. The kingdom of God would *not* come from among the Pharisees, and it would *not* come in the violent manner of Joshua, David, and Judah Maccabaeus. In fact, the kingdom of God *had* come, it *was* present, and it was happening in all

---

* John 3:1–21

that Jesus was doing. Jesus announced this over and over. But it would take a deep and profound rethinking of everything in order to see it—a radical reevaluation that would be a spiritual rebirth.

And not much has changed. You still have to be born again in the sense of undertaking a profound rethinking of dominant paradigms in order to see the kingdom of God. Without a willingness to take it from the top and rethink cherished assumptions, you can miss the kingdom of God as it breaks into the world. This was the great challenge the Pharisees faced—to recognize the kingdom of God as it was *actually happening* and not miss it because it was not as they imagined it would be.

> Once Jesus was asked by the Pharisees when the kingdom of God was coming, and he answered, "The kingdom of God is not coming with things that can be observed; nor will they say, 'Look, here it is!' or 'There it is!' For, in fact, the kingdom of God is among you."
>
> —LUKE 17:20–21

Jesus was telling the Pharisees, "You keep asking when the kingdom of God is going to come, but it's already here! You just haven't seen it." Jesus was telling the Pharisees that the future had arrived with what he was doing and with what was happening among his disciples. But you have to be born again to see it. It takes new eyes. Those who have been born again and have new eyes have seen the kingdom of God—they have, in fact, seen the future. Not only that, but also Jesus told Nicodemus that by being born of water (baptism) and the Spirit (regeneration) we can enter the kingdom of

God...now!* So as a baptized believer, this is my confession: I am from the future. I have seen and tasted the powers of the age to come.†

I am from the future, and I have seen where this thing (human history) is headed. I've seen the future that belongs to the age to come. I have seen the future in the lives of those who have seen the truth, who have believed in Jesus, who have been baptized into Christ, who have escaped the matrix of Babylon's dominant paradigm of power, lust, and greed and who are now living in the new realities of faith, hope, and love. I have seen the future because I am from the future. Paul describes it like this: "So if anyone is in Christ, there is a new creation: everything old has passed away; see, everything has become new!"‡ Paul isn't so much saying that the person in Christ is a new creation (the pronoun "he" is not in the text), but rather when a person is in Christ, they have already entered into God's new creation! Paul is saying, "Those who are in Christ belong to a brand-new world!" This is astounding, mysterious, and beautiful! Let me try to explain how it works.

The Christian faith is not a theology or a philosophy (though both a theology and a philosophy can be derived from it). Christianity is a *story*. It is a meta-narrative. It is a grand over-arching story that enables us to make sense of human history. It is the story of how God is setting right a world gone wrong and doing it through Jesus Christ. It is the story that starts with Creation in Genesis and takes us all the way through to new creation in Revelation. It is a story with Jesus Christ at the center of it. In a postmodern world devoid of any framing

---

\* John 3:5
† Hebrews 6:5
‡ 2 Corinthians 5:17

133

narrative that can make sense of the world, the Christian story offers the narrative of hope. This is the story we find ourselves a part of. When we believe the story (the gospel) and enter into it by baptism, we become participants in the story. And this story has a definite end in view. It is a story with an eschatology, an appointed end. The apostle Peter speaks of this eschatology as the restoration of all things.* The apostle Paul proclaims a new creation and tells of Jesus handing the restored kingdom back to God.† John the Revelator talks about a New Jerusalem and all things made new.‡ The end of the Christian story is beautiful. It is the beautiful "they lived happily ever after" culmination we long for. It's the true hope that myths and fairy tales allude to. It is restoration, new creation, the New Jerusalem, and all things made new. This is what we mean when we say Christianity is eschatological. The end is important, because it determines how we should act within the present as we head toward an appointed future. So we must be absolutely clear about this—the eschatological hope of Christianity is restoration and new creation.

But the end of the story the Bible tells is an end that has been inaugurated. That is to say, it is an end that has already begun. Thus theologians speak of "inaugurated eschatology." This simply means that the end has already been initiated. It means that when we confess, "Jesus is Lord," we are saying that Jesus has been inaugurated as the ruler of the world to bring about the end appointed by God—the restoration of all things. We must be careful that when we make the seminal Christian confession of "Jesus is Lord," we don't in actuality mean that

---

\*   Acts 3:21
†   2 Corinthians 5:17; 1 Corinthians 15:24
‡   Revelation 21; 22

he is "Lord-Elect." We speak of a newly elected president who has not yet been inaugurated and who has not yet taken office as "President-Elect." Jesus is not "Lord-Elect"; Jesus is Lord! Now! Jesus has been inaugurated, and he has taken office! He has ascended to the throne of God and sits at the right hand of the Father as the reigning ruler of the nations. Unless we see this clearly—and this is essential Christian orthodoxy— we will end up thinking that because Jesus has not yet taken office, we need to take it upon ourselves to run the world. No! Jesus *is* Lord! And if you say, "But it doesn't look like it," I will say, "Now faith is the assurance of things hoped for, the conviction of things not seen."* Nothing is more central to the Christian faith than our confession of "Jesus is Lord!" And this confession must form our eschatology.

This is why Peter and Paul explicitly say we are in the last days. The last days began with the resurrection of Jesus Christ, his ascension to the right hand of God, and the outpouring of the Holy Spirit upon the church on the Day of Pentecost. So am I saying that we are in the last days and we have been in the last days for two thousand years? Precisely. This is why Paul speaking to the Corinthian believers in the first century refers to them as those "on whom the ends of the ages have come."† With the resurrection of Jesus, the end of the ages has come. We are now living between the twilight of the old age and the dawn of the age to come. When Jesus rose from the dead, it was the beginning of the end for the age of sin and death. The apostle John says it like this: "The darkness is passing away and the true light is already shining."‡ X

twilight stage X

---

* Hebrews 11:1 *faith*
† 1 Corinthians 10:11
‡ 1 John 2:8 X

135

But here is the mystery: it's not as simple as one age ends and a new age begins. Some things that belong to the age to come have already been inaugurated, most notably Jesus being raised from the dead. This is why Paul speaks of the resurrection of Christ as the "firstfruits" or what we might call an "early harvest" of what is to come—the resurrection of the dead and the restoration of all things.* Even more mysteriously, Paul tells us that we who have believed and been baptized have already entered into the reality of new creation and the age to come! We are from the future! We live in the overlap of ages. We live in the tension between the now and not yet. We cannot say the kingdom has fully arrived, but we dare not say the kingdom has not come. Yes, the kingdom has come, and we are from the future! If we are regenerated by the Spirit and baptized into Christ, we are from the future. I know it sounds cute and clever, and we can make all kinds of jokes about *Back to the Future*—the flux capacitor, 1.21 gigawatts, 88 mph, and "Great Scott, Marty!"—but it's true; we are from the future.

But what does this mean? It means that by faith and baptism we have departed the age dominated by sin and death and stepped into the age to come—the age where Jesus is Lord and restores all things. As believers—and the word *believer* is critical for we are those who believe what is not yet seen—we are to anticipate the age to come *by living it now!* This lies at the heart of what it means to be a people who live by faith. Because we believe that Jesus is risen from the dead and that we will join him in resurrection, we are to by faith live in the

---

* See Romans 8; 1 Corinthians 15.

realities of resurrection here and now. Or, as Wendell Berry says it, we are to "practice resurrection."[1] Paul says it like this:

> For the grace of God has appeared, bringing salvation to all, training us to renounce impiety and worldly passions, and in the present age to live lives that are self-controlled, upright, and godly, while we wait for the blessed hope and the manifestation of the glory of our great God and Savior, Jesus Christ.
>
> —TITUS 2:11–13

Paul is saying that we who are in Christ should demonstrate the realities of the age to come by living them now in this present age. In the twilight of the age of sin and death, we are to cast off the works of sin and death and manifest the works of restoration and new creation that belong to the age to come. As the old age characterized by rebellion to God passes away, we are to anticipate the age to come by living lives of radical obedience to the Lord Jesus Christ here and now. It is in this way that we are a prophetic people. We are not a prophetic people by acting like a band of psychics making predictions about future events that belong to this age; we are a prophetic people when we bear prophetic witness to the age to come by living it here and now. To be in sync with the age to come is to be out of sync with the present age. It's what Nietzsche called *prophetic untimeliness*. The person who is truly prophetic is always out of step with the present age.

The church is to live as a prophetic people, not by predicting future events in the contemporary geopolitical context, but by being a prophetic witness of the age to come.

We are not prophetic by trying to predict Armageddon—we are prophetic by being a living, breathing prophecy of that righteous and peaceable government that is to come. Because we have entered into the reality of the kingdom of Christ through faith and baptism, we come from the future to show the people of this present age what is to come, where this is headed, what the future holds, and to invite them to join us.

It's in this manner that the apostles preached the gospel in the Book of Acts. Today we tend to think of preaching the gospel as something like this: *Jesus died for your sins to save you from hell. Make Jesus your Lord and Savior so you won't go to hell when you die.* It can be elaborated upon and made more eloquent, but that is basically the "gospel" as we hear it preached in the American evangelical church today. The only problem is that this bears virtually no resemblance to the gospel the apostles preached in the Book of Acts. It's not that the claim of the contemporary "gospel" is untrue; it's just not the way the apostles preached the gospel. Check it for yourself. There are about ten sermons in the Book of Acts (depending on what you count as a sermon), and none of them make an appeal to an afterlife or center salvation on escaping hell. None of them! Rather their gospel took on the form of an imperial proclamation (which is what *euaggelion* actually is). Their gospel proclamation was basically this: *The world now has a new Lord. It is Jesus the Christ. The proof of this is that God raised him to life again after the principalities and powers of this age put him to death on a cross. All who believe this proclamation and confess Jesus as Lord are forgiven of their sins. Now, rethink your life and act accordingly.* It wasn't a matter of "making Jesus Lord"—God had already made Jesus Lord! It was a matter of acknowledging this proclamation and acting accordingly (which is what repentance is all about).

Responding to the gospel is not a matter of obtaining a

ticket to enter the kingdom of heaven when you die but of acknowledging that the kingdom of heaven has already come through Jesus Christ and of living according to his righteous government here and now! This is why in the first gospel sermon in the Book of Acts (the sermon Peter gave on the Day of Pentecost) the "invitation" was not, "Be saved from hell," but, "Save yourselves from this corrupt generation."* In other words, Peter was calling people to stop living under the dominion of the principalities and powers of this age that are corrupting the world, and begin to live under the dominion of the world's new and rightful king—the Lord Jesus Christ. The apostles were announcing that in Christ the world has a new Emperor. (Which is, of course, why the apostles found themselves imprisoned and executed.) Peter and Paul were not sentenced to death by Caesar for telling people they could go to heaven when they die. They were executed for announcing the reign of a new Emperor! As the early Christian communities began to live lives that demonstrated the reign of the world's new Emperor—Jesus Christ—they were a prophetic people bearing witness to the age to come. They were from the future!

This is how the church bears prophetic witness to the world: by being a preview of what is to come. Think about when you go to a movie—before the feature film you are shown a series of trailers or "previews" of movies that will come to the theater in the future. You've probably seen hundreds of them—a three- or four-minute preview of a movie that will soon be in the theater. It's not the whole movie, but it's enough to give you an idea of what the future movie is about and what it will

---

\*   Acts 2:40

be like. So you could say the preview is *from the future*. That is precisely what the church is to be in this present age! We are to be a preview of what is to come. We are to be a partial preview of the full manifestation of the reign of Jesus Christ. The larger society should be able to look at the church and get an idea of where this thing is headed. The world should be able to look at the church and see a preview of what is to come. Of course this requires radical faithfulness on the part of the church. We are only from the future so long as we live lives of deep obedience to the lordship of Christ. If we are merely a religious version of the shared cultural assumptions of our age, we are chaplains to the status quo and no longer a prophetic people. What is most needed from the church in this age is that we recover our prophetic vocation and truly live as those who are from the future.

Because we are called to be from the future and thus a prophetic witness to the world, the first job of the church is not to be "relevant" or "successful" (which can easily become idols of compromise and accommodation). Instead, our primary task is to be *faithful*. Our greatest act of prophecy is to be loyal to the lordship of Jesus Christ here and now—to live as though we *actually believe* that Jesus is Lord! In order to be a prophetic people critiquing the present order and foretelling the future, we have to live as though we believe Jesus really is King of kings and Lord of lords. Or, to use contemporary vernacular, we are to live as though Jesus is the world's true President and permanent Prime Minister. Instead of imagining that Jesus's administration is relegated to a different space called *heaven* or a different time called *the future*, we are to live under his administration on earth and in the present time. We are to be living the answer to the prayer: "Thy government come; thy policy be done on earth as it is in heaven."

For the church to live according to its prophetic vocation, there is an essential question we need to be constantly asking: *What will the world to come look like?* We need to think seriously on this question. We need to allow the Holy Spirit and Scripture to inspire our imagination and catch a glimpse of what the Bible calls "the world to come."* We need to seriously discuss among ourselves what the world will look like when the end of the age arrives and Jesus "hands over the kingdom to God the Father, after he has destroyed every ruler and every authority and power."† What does the redemptive future of restored humanity look like? We need to ask this question, because once we obtain some idea of what the future for a world redeemed by Christ looks like, we have gained our course of action. What we are to do is anticipate the future by *living that way now!* To do this we need to ask ourselves things like: What will be abolished? What will be maintained? What will be restored? Having derived a vision by grappling with these questions, we need to then work for the abolition, maintenance, and restoration of these things. Which is to say we need to live under the administration (lordship) of Christ right now! We need to be from the future! Now! We must not compromise with the spirit of the age by saying something like, "Well, it's impossible to fully experience the reign of Christ now, so we might as well acquiesce with the principalities and powers." This is a renunciation of our prophetic vocation and disloyalty to our King.

Perhaps the best way to see how this works is to look at an

---

\* Hebrews 2:5, ESV, et al.

† 1 Corinthians 15:24

example from the past. Consider what was once a very controversial issue in American culture and the evangelical church—slavery. Today virtually no one views slavery as compatible with Christian ethics or would think of justifying slavery in a Christian context. But this has not always been the case. For generations "God-fearing," churchgoing Christians in the American South supported, justified, and even practiced slavery. How could this be? How could good "Bible-believing" Christians in apparent sincerity defend slavery as compatible with Christian ethics? The answer to the question is important.

First we need to acknowledge the Bible does *not* give a clear-cut prohibition of slavery—not in the Old Testament or even in the New Testament. If we think of the Bible as "God's Big Answer Book," we run into problems. The Bible does *not* have all the answers. This is evident when we consider slavery. Though we may find it embarrassing, and skeptics often point this out, the Bible indeed does not issue an unequivocal condemnation of slavery. And there are other similar examples. Why is this? Quite simply, the Bible is not that kind of book. To think of the Bible as an almanac or law book is a fundamentally wrong way of thinking about the Bible. The Bible doesn't provide all the answers in a legalistic sense for two primary reasons. First, it would be practically impossible—the Bible would have to contain millions of pages. (Have you ever seen a law library?!) Second, and perhaps more important, such a use of Scripture is entirely contrary to God's intention to create free, rational, thinking beings that bear his image. Christianity is *not* about rules! That's moralism. That's Pharisaism. Christianity is about the life of Christ imparted to the human race. The Bible doesn't give us all the answers, but it does provide us with a structure for renewing our minds.

Simply put, the Bible can teach us to _think_. As we learn to think in a Christlike manner, we can begin to discern the will of God. But if all we want to do is "paint by numbers" with the Bible...well, most recognize that it's possible to "biblically" justify almost anything with a concordance and a bit of cleverness. It's been done many times. Killing, polygamy, hatred, racism, sexism, slavery, war, witch hunts, crusades, and genocide have all been justified by people "using" the Bible. The escaped slave, social reformer, and Christian abolitionist Frederick Douglass had seen the Bible used to sanction even the most cruel aspects of slavery.

> I have seen him [my master] tie up a lame young woman, and whip her with a heavy cowskin upon her naked shoulders, causing the warm red blood to drip; and, in justification of the bloody deed, he would quote this passage of Scripture—"He that knoweth his master's will, and doeth it not, shall be beaten with many stripes."[2]

In 1844 a controversy arose in the Methodist church concerning the issue of slavery. The controversy came to a head over a slave-owning bishop in Georgia. Most Northern Methodists insisted that the slave-owning bishop resign, while Southern Methodists defended the right of the bishop to own slaves. (The proslavery fear was that if a bishop could be condemned for slave ownership, the entire institution of slavery could fall under condemnation.) In May of 1844, one hundred eighty Methodist delegates gathered in New York in an attempt to settle the matter. Here are some of the transcripts of arguments presented by the proslavery pastors and bishops:[3]

"You cannot, brethren, lay your finger on a text that says no man can hold slaves and be a Christian."

"Slavery was established decree of Almighty God. It is sanctioned in the Bible, in both Testaments, from Genesis to Revelation."

"Moreover, of the children of the strangers that do sojourn among you, of them shall ye buy, and they shall be your possession. They shall be your bondmen forever. Leviticus chapter 25, verses 45 and 46."

"It appears plain to me why this epistle [Philemon] has been preserved. It is that men may see that it is possible to hold slaves and go to heaven."

There you have it. According to the proslavery Methodist pastors, slavery was a divine institution sanctioned by God and blessed in the Bible. They could cite chapter and verse to "prove" it. After two weeks of impassioned and often acrimonious debate, the matter was put to a vote. Predictably the vote broke down along North and South lines. One hundred ten Northern Methodists demanded the slave-owning bishop resign, while sixty-eight Southern Methodists voted in support of the bishop. A year later the Southern Methodist churches broke away and formed the Methodist Episcopal Church South. Other Protestant denominations suffered similar splits over the issue of slavery. Thus the conservative, Bible-believing churches in the American South continued as worshiping communities while perfectly at home with slavery. They had lost their prophetic voice and become religious cheerleaders for the principalities and powers. They were chaplains of the status quo. They were priests of the present age. It was this kind of smug, self-satisfied, self-serving accommodating Christianity that Frederick Douglass as a prophet to the nation so severely and eloquently denounced.

> Between the Christianity of this land, and the Christianity of Christ, I recognize the widest possible difference.... The slave auctioneer's bell and the church-going bell chime in with each other.... The slave prison and the church stand near each other.[4]

The conservative Southern churches playing a paint-by-numbers game with the Bible and comfortable with the status quo got it wrong. But what could they have done to get it right? They only needed to ask one question to arrive at the correct answer: *In the coming age, will slavery be maintained or abolished?* The conservative Southern churches acquiesced with slavery because, as they would have said, "it's just the way things are." Their whole system and standard of living were dependent upon slavery. They understood their economy was fueled by slave labor, and so they were determined to preserve it. Instead of allowing their thinking to be formed by Christ, they employed the Bible as a propaganda tool to serve their agenda. But not even the proslavery Christians of the American South would have argued that slavery was eternal or that slaves of this age were fated to remain slaves forever. They would not have believed that slaves on earth were slaves in heaven. They simply believed that heaven and earth were (fortunately for them) far apart. For the proslavery Christians of the American South, the redemptive future had no bearing on the present. They were from the present. They were not prophetic. They were entirely time confined to their own age. They were *not* from the future. And it was a tragedy.

I would like for you to engage in a thought experiment. It

will require the use of some imagination. The first thing I want you to imagine is a time machine. Maybe it's Doc Brown's DeLorean or Doctor Who's TARDIS or a time machine of your own creation. You need a time machine because you are being sent on a mission that will take you back in time. You are being sent to Montgomery, Alabama, in 1850. Your task is to go to the First Conservative Church of Montgomery and convince them to change their position on slavery. Good luck.

So how would you go about it? What would you say? I would suggest that you simply tell the truth. Tell them you are from the future. Tell them about the future. Be prophetic. Tell them about a coming war that will be horrible beyond imagining. Tell them about a tall man born in a log cabin in Kentucky. Tell them about an Emancipation Proclamation. Tell them about a Fourteenth Amendment and the wrongs it will right. Perhaps you could take them much farther into the future and tell them other things. Tell them about a woman from their own town who will become famous because she won't give up her seat on a bus. Tell them about a preacher from Atlanta named after the man who launched the Protestant Reformation who will one day be a pastor in their city. Tell them about this great man's dream. Tell them how he will die a martyr's death and change a nation. Tell them where the future is headed. You might even tell them about the first African American president (and then give them CPR!).

You might say it like this: "My dear Christian friends, I am from the future. I am a prophetic witness of that which is to come. The future does not belong to you. The future does not belong to your system. The future does not belong to slavery. Slavery has no future. And if you continue to align yourself with that which is destined to be abolished, the future will hold you in contempt. The future belongs to emancipation. The future belongs to equality. The future belongs to dignity. The future belongs to justice. And now I call you to rethink everything you have assumed, because the time for change is upon you; the future is at hand. I call you to anticipate and bless the coming future by embracing it now!" You would not accept the excuses of the slavery-endorsing Christians who might say something like, "Slavery will change when Jesus comes back, but for now this is just the way things are; for now slavery is necessary." You would not accept that! You would say, "No! The time for abolition is now! The future is upon you! You must change now!"

If you were to preach such a message, you would in essence be saying, "Repent! For the kingdom of heaven is at hand!" And you would be lucky to make it out alive. But perhaps some would hear you. Perhaps some would believe. Perhaps some would believe that you are from the future and respond to your prophetic message by rethinking their lives, freeing their slaves, and helping them to recover the inherent dignity that belongs to their humanity. Those who did so might very well lose everything. It would not be a "practical" or "reasonable" or "successful" thing to do, but it would be the prophetic and faithful thing to do. Those acting on your word would be entering the kingdom of heaven in the present. But it would be as the apostle Paul described it to the fledgling congregations in Syria: "It is through many persecutions that we must enter the kingdom of God."* Indeed the kingdom of God never comes in a new way without those who are committed to the present age persecuting those who are from the future.

---

* Acts 14:22

To be a prophetic witness to the kingdom of God nearly always requires passing through some kind of tribulation, for the simple reason that the principalities and powers do not easily cede their positions of privilege.

The Southern writer Lillian Smith was a prophetic voice who found out how unpopular a person can become if they are from the future. Lillian Smith was born in the Deep South in 1897, a time and place not far removed from slavery—racism was the order of the day and society was still rigidly segregated. Jim Crow laws made African Americans second-class citizens. In 1944 Smith's first novel, *Strange Fruit*, was published and became an instant best seller. It sold three million copies, was translated into fifteen languages, and was made into a Broadway play. Five years later Smith published her second book, *Killers of the Dream*. This book was not a follow-up novel but an exposé of the sins of the South and a call for the civil rights of all people. It was shocking and "affronted too many southerners—including powerful moderates—to be financially or critically successful.... This subject matter and Smith's innovative style were met with hostility, or deliberate silence, by the literary establishment, the New Critics, and the general public of Cold War America."[5] Here is a sample of Smith's untimely prophetic critique of the pre-Civil Rights South:

> The mother who taught me what I know of tenderness and love and compassion taught me also the bleak rituals of keeping Negroes in their "place." The father who rebuked me for an air of superiority toward schoolmates from the mill and rounded out his rebuke by gravely reminding me that "all men are

brothers," trained me in the steel-rigid decorums I must demand of every colored male....

I learned it is possible to be a Christian and a white southerner simultaneously; to be a gentlewoman and an arrogant callous creature in the same moment; to pray at night and ride a Jim Crow car the next morning and to feel comfortable in doing both. I learned to believe in freedom, to glow when the word democracy was used, and to practice slavery from morning to night. I learned it the way all my southern people learn it: by closing door after door until one's mind and heart and conscience are blocked off from each other and from reality.[6]

It took tremendous courage and deep conviction to write those words in 1949 America—words that were hated and unheeded and that nearly cost Lillian Smith her literary career. But a decade later *Killers of the Dream* provided inspiration for Martin Luther King Jr., whose dream would not be killed—though the dreamer would be. Lillian Smith's career was wrecked and Martin Luther King's life was taken for the same reason—they were from the future.

As we in our own time imagine by faith the world to come, we are helped by the prophets. Assisting our imagination in rethinking the world is a primary task of the poet-prophets. They give us their prophetic metaphors to help us untether our imagination from the tyranny of the status quo. None do it better than Isaiah of the Exile. His poetic portrayal of a future framed by holiness and bearing the fruit of peace is what inspired Handel and the countless others who have dared to dream of a better world. In his song Isaiah sings of a future where idolatry and violence give way to true worship and neighborliness. This is the beautiful portrait of eschatological hope given to us in the second half of Isaiah (chapters 40–66). Isaiah's hopeful future of redemption and restoration is what Joseph of Arimathea was waiting for and what Jesus inaugurated and what the return of Christ will consummate. It is the future that we are to believe in, belong to, and move toward. It is the music from that distant land where the lion lies down with the lamb that we are to hear and dance to even now. Why? Because we are from the future.

 Our first priority as the church is not to make all these things happen in the world through political action, but to be a prophetic witness to the hope of a world remade according to Christ. Every redemptive action—political and otherwise—must proceed from our faithful witness. In the midst of a hateful, violent, and idolatrous world, the church is to be an enclave of love, peace, and holiness. To be a faithful church, the church must be distinguished by holiness. Not holiness as puritanical moralism, but holiness as *otherness*—we are to be *other* to the values of this present darkness. Christian holiness is not based upon a certain set of rules but upon the fact that we are from another time. If we approach holiness as a legislative issue, we are prone to get it wrong. And even if we are not wrong in our judgment, we are likely to be ugly about it—haughty, condemning, and condescending. Holiness is not that. Holiness is not moralism. Holiness is not legalism. Holiness is not puritanical rule keeping. Holiness is otherness. Holiness is prophetic untimeliness. Holiness is the transcendent beauty that comes from belonging to the redemptive future. Holiness is a preview of the world to come. Holiness is a picture of the beauty that is to be. To live now according to the beauty that shall be because the future belongs to God is what the psalmist means when he calls upon us to "worship the LORD in the beauty of holiness."* We are holy when we are other. We are holy when we transcend the dominant paradigms of present corruption. We are holy when we are from the future.

In his epistle to the Romans the apostle Paul appealed to the Christians living in Rome not to live according to their old pagan identity framed by the empire, but to live out of their new baptismal identity. Christian baptism conveys a new identity; baptism is not a mere symbol but a sacred portal. Baptism is a mystical portal to the future. The baptized have made their exodus from the present age and now belong to the world to come. Like Israel leaving their old slave identity in Egypt and passing through the waters of the Red Sea to gain a new identity in a promised land, so the Christian passes through the waters of baptism to gain a new identity in the world to come. This is why the early Christians had the practice of giving new names to converts at the time of their baptism. This is where the concept of your "given" name or "Christian" name originates. A Christian name is the name of baptismal identity. Imagine a young pagan woman living in Rome in the first century. Her name is Invidia. It's a Roman name. It's the name of the goddess of retribution. But Invidia hears the imperial proclamation (*euaggelion*) about the new Emperor, Jesus Christ. She believes the gospel and is saved. At her baptism Invidia takes a new name. Perhaps she is given the name Christa because she no longer confesses Caesar as Lord but now confesses Christ as Lord. The girl formally known as Invidia is no more. She is now Christa. She will tell her friends to call her by her new name, the name of her

---

\* Psalm 29:2, KJV

baptismal identity. It is this baptismal identity that Paul calls the Roman Christians to live out of when he says:

> What then are we to say? Should we continue in sin in order that grace may abound? By no means! How can we who died to sin go on living in it? Do you not know that all of us who have been baptized into Christ Jesus were baptized into his death? Therefore we have been buried with him by baptism into death, so that, just as Christ was raised from the dead by the glory of the Father, so we too might walk in newness of life.
>
> —ROMANS 6:1–4

Upon her baptism, Christa passed from the old world and into the new. She departed a world of corruption that is fading away and entered into the eternal world to come. Christa is now from the future. For Christa, holiness is not based upon legalistic rule keeping but upon the fact that she is now living in a new empire—she is now living under the Emperor Christ. Invidia lived according to the cultural assumptions of the Roman Empire, but Christa now lives according to the newness of life found in Christ. Christa is saved because she no longer belongs to that which has been condemned and is passing away; she now belongs to that which is to come and will remain. Christa is from the future, and she is living according to eternal life.

What is true of our imaginary first-century Christian is true of every contemporary Christian. Our baptism proclaims that we are from the future. We have passed from death to life. We have renounced the ways and means of domination and death. Baptism is our "naturalization ceremony" where we transfer our allegiance and loyalty from the kingdom of this world to the kingdom of heaven. We are now citizens of New Jerusalem. We carry the passport of that kingdom whose coming beautifully remakes all that is ugly in our world. We are a colony of life in the country of death. As colonists, we are to bring the life, culture, and beauty of Christ's kingdom into the shadowlands of decay. We are to practice resurrection. As Eugene Peterson puts it: "The practice of resurrection is...an open invitation to live eternity in time."[7]

We are from the future. In a world motivated by the primal lusts for money, sex, and power, we are to be a prophetic witness of a future motivated by love. We reject greed, immorality, and domination, not so much because they are "against the rules," but because the future belongs to love. The masters of suspicion are most suspicious of love. Marx says it's all about money. Freud says it's all about sex. Nietzsche says it's all about power. All three ultimately reject the validity of love. But we are to prove the masters of suspicion wrong. Jesus says it's all about love—and we are called to prove that Jesus is right! We do it by living here and now as a people motivated, not by money, sex, and power, but by love.

We are from the future. In a world being torn apart by hate and hostility we are a prophetic witness to the peaceable kingdom of Christ. We reject a warring mentality because we believe and confess that Jesus has already conquered and is already reigning as Lord. "What is wrong with the world is most fundamentally that people respond to evil with evil."[8] Revenge doesn't work. Because we believe that Jesus is Lord and rules the nations from the right hand of the Father, we see the temptation to respond to evil with evil and to violence with violence as unbelief and rebellion to the lordship of Christ.

We are from the future. In a world devoid of imagination and dominated by *the way it's always been*, we are to be a prophetic witness to *otherness* and holy imagination. We reject the pretentious claims of the principalities and powers that the way the world is presently arranged is the way it has to be. The principalities and powers committed to the status quo say that poverty is inevitable, that war is unavoidable, and the exploitation of the weak by the strong is inescapable. But we refuse to acquiesce to all of that. Why? Because we have heard the song of the prophets. We have seen the vision that John saw. We have believed the gospel the apostles proclaimed. We have confessed that Jesus Christ is Lord. We have an imagination inspired by the Holy Spirit, and we believe in the world to come.

We are from the future. We are persuaded that the future belongs to beauty. Beauty will save the world. The beauty of Christ will save the world from the ugliness of greed, violence, domination, idolatry, and immorality. We believe this. So we seek to "behold the beauty of the Lord"* and reflect that beauty back into our broken world. We do this in the hope that broken humanity will catch a glimpse of the beauty that is to be, believe in that beauty, and call upon our beautiful Savior.

---

* Psalm 27:4

## CHAPTER 6

# A CATHEDRAL OF
# ASTONISHMENT

The Gospel of Mark was the first of the four Gospels to be written, and its original ending was rather strange and quite abrupt. At a later date a longer and more satisfying ending was appended, but Mark's original conclusion to his Gospel narrative was simply this: "And they went out and fled from the tomb, for trembling and astonishment had seized them, and they said nothing to anyone, for they were afraid."* The End. But how can that be the end? It's so sudden, so abrupt, so lacking in resolution or explanation. We're left with three women fleeing from the empty tomb, trembling, astonished, and speechless. It's as if the film in the projector simply ran out, and we find ourselves sitting in the theater puzzled by the unexpected ending.

Perhaps it is helpful to think of Mark's Gospel as a movie. Let's try. As Jesus dies on the cross at the end of chapter—or

---

* Mark 16:8, ESV

shall we say "scene"—fifteen, the camera lingers on Christ, now dead, but still hanging on the cross. Even in death Christ preserves the posture of the cruciform—his arms remain outstretched in an endless offer of embrace. The infinite act of forgiveness is frozen in finite form. But now the camera pans away from the cross and focuses on three women who are standing a respectful distance from the cross and who through their tears have seen the hope they placed in the prophet from Galilee come to a bitter end as Jesus breathed his last. They are Mary Magdalene, Mary the mother of James, and Salome. In a tender act of devotion, these three women maintain a vigil with the body of Jesus as Joseph of Arimathea obtains permission from Pontius Pilate to bury Jesus in his own nearby tomb. Mary Magdalene, the other Mary, and Salome follow Joseph and Nicodemus as they carry the body of Jesus to the burial site. They watch as Jesus is placed in the tomb and witness the stone rolled against the entrance as the sun sets on this long, sad Friday. Fade to black. End of scene fifteen.

Scene sixteen opens with the same three women on their way to the tomb very early on Sunday morning. The sun is not yet risen, and the world still lies mostly in shadows. They are bringing spices to add to the body of Jesus as a final act of devotion. Their conversation is in hushed whispers and is mostly about the dilemma of how to remove the large stone from the entrance to the tomb. Entering the gate into Joseph's walled garden, they make their way to the tomb. Because of the darkness of the early hour, they are almost upon the tomb before they realize—to their alarm—that the stone sealing the tomb has been rolled back. Trying to understand what has happened, they enter the tomb, and now things become even stranger. They are more than startled as they find a young man in a white robe sitting inside the tomb. The stranger speaks to them, saying, "Do not be alarmed. You seek Jesus of Nazareth, who was crucified. He has risen; he is not here. See the place where they laid him. But go, tell his disciples and Peter that he is going before you to Galilee. There you will see him, just as he told you."* That's when the three women run out of the tomb and flee from the garden, trembling, astonished, and speechless. The movie ends. Roll the credits. What a strange way to end a movie—or a Gospel.

Yet this was the original ending to Mark's Gospel. Fear, trembling, and astonished silence. Of course we understand why eventually the need was felt to add a more thorough ending (seventeen additional verses) as the other Gospels do. There needed to be a further explanation of the empty tomb. Christian theology in its essence is the extrapolation of implications based on the resurrection of Jesus Christ. The Gospel of John, the last of the Gospels to be written, has two full chapters following the resurrection. There is much to be written about, thought out, worked out; in fact, this is what the New Testament epistles are—the outworking of resurrection implications.

But!...Mark's original ending was the perfect way to the end the first Gospel, if only for a while. Three women make a startling discovery that leaves them trembling, astonished, and speechless. Perfect. Astonishment, accompanied by fear and trembling, evoking stunned silence *should* be our first response to the gospel! Just think how unsatisfactory it would have been if Mary Magdalene had calmly said, "Oh, yes, this makes perfect sense"—and then gone on to give the other two

---

* Mark 16:6–7, ESV

women some erudite explanation like a German theologian giving a university lecture. As the Romanian-French playwright Eugene Ionesco understood, "Explanation separates us from astonishment, which is the only gateway to the incomprehensible."[1] If explanation had been the first response to the resurrection, something would have been wrong. And something *is* wrong!

What's wrong is that we have precious little astonishment in our gospel. We're familiar with it. It's become old hat. It's in danger of degenerating into cliché. It's anything but astonishing. It has only the faux astonishment of a late-night infomercial. *For only $19.95! But wait, there's more! Call now! Operators are standing by!* We yawn and change the channel. I'm afraid that's how our gospel is too often heard. But consider how the gospel sounded upon its first hearing in the first century. A Galilean Jew named Jesus was executed by crucifixion for alleged crimes against the state by the Roman government; three days later God raised him from the dead, and he is now the world's new emperor. That's the gospel! It's not an explanation; it's an announcement. It's the surprising announcement that a crucified Galilean Jew has risen from the dead and is now the world's new ruler! It may sound absurd, but it's certainly not cliché. No matter what else one might say about this gospel, it is certainly an astonishing claim.

But in our day the sense of astonishment is largely absent. We don't think of the gospel as an absurd claim, though it is! (Which is not to say it isn't true!) In our modern sophistication and over-familiarity with the gospel, we have removed astonishment from the gospel. We have replaced astonishment with something a bit tamer. We have made the gospel reasonable, sensible, and practical. We explain the gospel in cogent terms like "the plan of salvation" and "spiritual laws"—as if it is simply the most rational thing in the world. The gospel is no longer astonishing; it is now commonsense, logical, and, most of all, "useful." We have no use for astonishment because, well, we have no *use* for astonishment. Astonishment is not something we can *use*—it's not something pragmatic that we can utilize to further our self-concocted and self-oriented agendas. So instead of announcing an astonishing gospel, we find ourselves trying to sell a useful gospel. Evangelism takes on the tone of a multilevel marketing presentation. Some buy it, some don't, but not many are astonished.

Yet astonishment is the most appropriate initial reaction to the gospel story. To respond to the gospel story (and it is a *story*, not a set of propositions) with calmly asked utilitarian questions is completely inappropriate—as if one were kicking the tires on a used car. What if the three women at the tomb on the first Easter had calmly responded to the angel with a series of consumerist questions like this: "What do I do with this?" "How do I use it?" "How can I make this practical in my life?"—as if the angel had just presented them a business plan. No! The first response must be astonishment and stunned silence. The gospel properly proclaimed and properly heard is a mystery evoking awe—not a prospectus eliciting calculation. Without astonishment as our initial response, we meet Christianity in a wrong way—or more properly, we meet *Christ* in a wrong way.

My own experience of encountering Jesus Christ as a teenager was absolutely astonishing—at least it was to me. It wasn't that I was previously unaware of the gospel or the "plan of salvation." Having grown up in an evangelical church, I was quite familiar with all of this. But then it happened. I encountered Christ. Out of the blue. It was the last thing I expected. To this day it remains a bit hard to explain, and anyway, attempts at explanation seem to diminish the experience into a kind of rational "decision" stripped of mystery. But it was mysterious, and it was astonishing. I, Brian Zahnd, a run-of-the-mill teenage Led Zeppelin freak from a real-life Mayberry in the Midwest, had met Jesus Christ in a mystical encounter! And it changed me. Everyone around me knew that something had happened. I turned into the school "Jesus freak." When my friends would say, "I can't believe what has happened to you," I would simply reply, "I can't either—but it has." Of course the tendency is to fit such an experience into a particular category. You could say I had been "saved" or had "made a decision for Christ" or had "become a Christian." But I had already done all that. I had already walked the aisle, prayed the prayer, and been baptized. There was never a time when I didn't believe in Jesus, at least in a theoretical sense. Yet what faith I possessed dwelt on the periphery of my life. But now something astonishing had happened, something that seemed to defy easy categorization. To this day I'm still not quite sure how to categorize what happened (as if categorization needs to be done!), other than to say I had an astonishing mystical encounter with Jesus Christ that profoundly changed me—and that will have to be enough. Søren Kierkegaard said, "When you label me, you negate me."[2] We can do the same thing with a spiritual experience—slap a label on it so you can set it aside. Experiences with God are not the same thing as catching, categorizing, and labeling butterflies.

All true faith, theology, and witness must first be preceded by genuine astonishment or it will be trivialized. Without astonishment we inevitably reduce the gospel to inert "ology" and "ism." Or worse yet, it becomes a spiritual "product" that we must "market." This is consumer Christianity, and it is the bane of our age. The line between the televangelist and tele-marketer is a thin one indeed. We unblushingly speak of "marketing" the gospel. We see nothing contradictory in it. Perhaps we actually believe the gospel *is* a kind of product. God help us! What is needed is astonishment! We need to be so aston-ished that it silences us for a season as it did Mary Magdalene and her friends. We need astonishment to save us from the encroaching pragmatism that threatens to take over evangel-ical Christianity. We need astonishment to rescue us from the cheap answers and easy-believism of a clichéd Christianity. Worship must originate in astonishment and proceed without agenda or it degenerates into mere entertainment. We end up evaluating "worship experiences" based on what it does for *us*. Something is wrong here. Furthermore, we don't want theolo-gians, pastors, teachers, or worship leaders (or, for that matter, Christians) who are not astonished by the absurd claims of the Incarnation and Resurrection. We need to once again be astonished like the three women on that first Easter—astonished, not by what the gospel can *do*, but astonished first of all for what it *is!*

Throughout the latter half of the twentieth century, and now into the twenty-first century, American evangelicals have increasingly touted the virtues of the gospel by promoting it as "practical." This has become something of an article of faith. It is unquestioned and fully assumed that we should "make the gospel practical." We advertise that our churches have "prac-tical" sermons. The goal of every sermon is to give a practical way of "applying it to your life" (which is why theological ser-mons on, say, the Trinity, are now anathema). We even speak of making the Bible "relevant." (How grateful God must be that someone has at last made his Word relevant!) But do we fail to see that this is the secular language of the market and not the sacred language of mystery? This is the language of consumerism, not the language of Christianity. This is the language of business, not the language of faith. As Eugene Peterson said in a recent conversation with pastors, "Salesmanship language is the common language of America, and it needs to be kept out of the pulpit." Of course the argument is, how are we going to get any takers if we don't sell the gospel on practical grounds? How indeed? Perhaps we will have to place some faith in the gospel and in Jesus Christ himself. Perhaps we will have to believe that the gospel story itself, faithfully told, still has the capacity to astonish. Perhaps we will have to believe that the risen Christ can still make himself known in astonishing ways.

The problem with pragmatism applied to Christianity is that it denudes the gospel of its inherent mystery. When we take it upon ourselves to explain the gospel so we can promote its benefits and get people to sign on, we unintentionally but inevitably diminish the mystery and beauty of the gospel. We turn the beauty that saves the world into a utility for self-improvement. But the language of utility is completely foreign to the New Testament. Christ and the apostles speak of mystery, not of utility. Hans Urs von Balthasar reminds us of something important when he says, "In the end, only something endowed with mystery is worthy of love. It is impossible to love something stripped of mystery; at best it would be a thing one uses as one sees fit."[3] I'm afraid that is what we have unwittingly done. Through our marketing techniques and pragmatic approach, we have removed the mystery and beauty from Christianity and turned it into a utility. We use it as we see fit, but we find it hard to be enraptured by it. Mystery is an irreplaceable factor in the equation of love. Just let a scientist try to explain love in terms of biological necessity and utilitarian function, and see what his explanation does to love—it destroys it. Authentic Christianity does not do this. Christianity is not a science; it is a faith—*the* faith. Christianity is a confession, not an explanation. We confess Christ; we don't explain Christ. We confess the Trinity, the Incarnation, the Resurrection, and the Ascension, though we cannot fully explain these mysteries. We leave room for mystery. We honor the mystery. We recognize the beauty in the mystery.

There is the honored Christian practice of what St. Anselm called "faith seeking understanding," but the point is we begin with faith, not with understanding or explanation. We begin with faith because faith is the confessional response to the mystery of divine revelation—and the initial human response to divine revelation is astonishment. We will always confess far more than we can explain. Of course the reality of revelation and the response of faith offend modern man with his blind faith in empiricism. So be it. Christianity cannot fit within the empirical limitations imposed by the Enlightenment. If we reduce the Christian faith to only that which we can explain, we end up with a paper-thin, watered-down, cheap knock-off of Christianity that no longer has the capacity to astonish.

Some years ago a girl from our church was on a youth mission trip to Spain, and while there she had an opportunity to visit the great Cathedral of Barcelona—La Seu. Construction on the Barcelona Cathedral was begun in 1298 and completed in 1448. La Seu is one of the great triumphs of medieval

Gothic architecture and still inspires worshipers and visitors today. Gothic architecture with its soaring arches, flying buttresses, ribbed vaults, and enormous stained-glass windows was designed to evoke an awareness of the transcendent and an overwhelming sense of awe in the worshiper. It was an architectural attempt to connect heaven and earth. The construction of these great cathedrals was itself an act of worship. Five and a half centuries after the completion of La Seu, a young American girl from an evangelical background had her first encounter with a great European Gothic cathedral. She described it to me like this.

> The ornate arcs caused my eyes to lift up, as if into heaven. The soft afternoon sunlight poured in through the stained glass. Dust particles floated timelessly through the hazy light. The depiction of Christ crucified came into focus. I felt as though my soul had transcended the earth. I wanted nothing more than to fall on my knees and worship in this ancient, beautiful, and holy place. Hot tears fell down my face.[4]

This American teenager was so overwhelmed by an encounter with sacred beauty that she was moved to tears. Why? She was astonished. Having grown up in the soulless strip mall plastic culture of American suburbia and its ubiquitous pragmatism, she suddenly had a devastating encounter with what we have lost—holy mystery and sacred beauty. An encounter with something wholly *other*, a Gothic cathedral, produced astonishment—and the astonishment expressed itself in awe and tears. In the Barcelona Cathedral, this young evangelical instinctively recognized—perhaps as a metaphor—that we have lost something, something we cannot really live without. We've lost mystery and beauty and the power they have to produce the kind of astonishment that naturally leads to worship. Sure, she knew about worship, but too much of what passes for worship today is merely a rally. Astonishment is replaced with manufactured enthusiasm. *Hip-hip, hooray!* But we need something more.

My point is not the obvious fact that a Gothic cathedral has a different effect upon our souls than a sterile big box store. I'm not really talking about architecture; I'm using it as a metaphor. What we need is the kind of Christianity that can produce in people the kind of astonishment that the Barcelona Cathedral produced in the American teenager. What we need in our faith, theology, and witness is to build a *cathedral of astonishment.* Or more accurately, we need to rediscover and preserve the cathedral of astonishment that is authentic Christianity when it is imbued with mystery and beauty.

In the American Christianity of the past fifty years we have built the equivalent of a big box store of pragmatism—a kind of discount God-Mart. But what we need is a cathedral of astonishment. Why? Because everything that makes up the essential framework of Christianity *is* astonishing! Consider: We confess a Trinity—one God who is Father, Son, and Holy Spirit. We believe in the mystery of the Incarnation—that the Word became flesh through a virgin birth. We proclaim that somehow God saves the world through the execution of a particular Jew outside the city of Jerusalem in the early first century. We preach that this crucified man—Jesus of Nazareth—has been raised from the dead. Furthermore, we confess that he has ascended to the right hand of the Father and now rules the nations as King of kings and Lord of lords. We believe he is coming again to judge the living and the dead. We believe that through Jesus Christ will come the resurrection of the dead and all things made new. Every bit of this is astonishing! Trinity, Incarnation, Resurrection, Ascension—these are our soaring arches, flying buttresses, ribbed vaults, and stained-glass windows. They are not practical; they are mysterious and beautiful!

Nothing about the essential creeds and central confessions of orthodox Christianity readily lend themselves to pragmatic self-improvement programs. Asking, "How do I apply the Trinity to my life so as to make it practical?," is simply asking the wrong kind of question. Once you approach the sacred mysteries of the Christian faith with a utilitarian agenda, you are never going to get a satisfactory response. It would be like asking the custodians of the Barcelona Cathedral, "How do I apply this to my life?" They wouldn't even understand the question.

To continue with the metaphor... Christianity is not a tool or a ticket or a talisman—it is a cathedral! You cannot use it or own it or possess it any more than you can use, own, or possess a Gothic cathedral. You can't put in your pocket like a wallet, a pocketknife, or a lucky penny—you can only enter it. Christianity is not something you "add to your life"; it is something you *enter*. And you enter it on its own terms, not yours. Christ is the door that leads to this astonishing cathedral called salvation. To enter into authentic Christianity is to leave the shrunken world of staid moralism and sterile pragmatism. It is to enter a kind of cathedral that is so big, so beautiful, so astonishing that worship is the only acceptable response. What I'm trying to say is that Christianity with its sacred mysteries is a grand and gorgeous cathedral—it is something much bigger and more beautiful than what we have become accustomed to in a stripped-down pragmatized Christianity sold on the cheap at the local God-Mart.

As Christians we are the heirs of a faith that has been  entrusted to us. We don't get to make God up or improvise a personal Christianity. We are not permitted to cobble together a homemade faith of our liking. Christianity is a *received* faith—we receive it from the witness of apostles, and it has been handed down to us through the ages. It is "the faith that was once for all entrusted to the saints."* We are not the architects of the faith; we are the trustees. Again, this is like an ancient cathedral—we didn't build it; we can only reverence it and preserve it. So before we attempt to explain the Trinity or Incarnation or Baptism or Communion, we must first reverence these holy mysteries by being astonished at them. Astonished silence precedes apostolic preaching. Without astonishment we lack reverence, and without reverence we are reckless. And we have been reckless with the received faith. In our reckless attempt to make Christianity popular by making it "practical," we invariably vandalize it by stripping it of its inherent beauty and mystery. So in North America we have a Christianity that is relatively popular but damaged. It is thin, shallow, and trite. We make it practical by adapting it to the assumed values of the wider culture. We figure out what people want, and then offer them a Christianized version of it. We do it in the name of church growth, but it is really the betrayal of a sacred trust. It would be like turning St. Paul's Cathedral into a shopping mall to increase traffic. But in the long run, when we sacrifice beauty and mystery for the sake of practicality, we paradoxically end up making it impractical. Think of all the abandoned

---

* Jude 3

strip malls that we no longer have any use for. That is the lesson: when we sacrifice the beautiful for the useful, we eventually end up with something entirely useless!

Oscar Wilde once said, "All art is quite useless."[5] Wilde meant this as praise for art. He meant that the value of art lay precisely in the fact that art is not something we can utilize. Art is not a tool. Beauty is not a utility. These are not things we can possess; yet there is a sense in which art and beauty are something we cannot live without. We crave the astonishment and sublime sense of satisfaction that beauty can bring to our lives. C. S. Lewis once said something to the effect that we don't need art to survive, but we need art to make survival worth the effort. Because art cannot be used in the conventional sense of the word, we confer upon it a kind of sacred status. To use art is exploitation. The great masterpieces are not utilized; they are revered. No one demands that Michelangelo's *David* be made practical in order to have value. The fact that we cannot "use" Michelangelo's *David* is intrinsic to the sacredness of the masterpiece. Likewise it is the sacrosanct beauty of the "useless" aspects of the Christian faith that make it invaluable and sacred.

What is distinct about Christianity is its sacred mysteries. Oprah and Dr. Phil and the rest of the apostles of self-improvement can give plenty of advice on how to deal with the problems in your life, but only Christianity confesses a Trinity, an Incarnation, and a Resurrection. If we abandon these sacred mysteries as superfluous to the goal of giving people something practical, we should not be surprised if eventually they abandon Christianity as superfluous to the pragmatic project of self-improvement. Instead of presenting Christianity as the latest gadget, we need to present it as an ancient cathedral. If we have no respect for the sacred mysteries of the faith and acquiesce to the American pressure to be practical—*What's the Trinity got to do with me finding success in life?*—we become like the Soviets who turned Russian cathedrals into warehouses. Failing to recognize the worth of beauty independent from utilitarian function is symptomatic of an abject poverty of the soul. It's like saying that if we turned St. Peter's Basilica into a parking garage, we would improve it by making it practical. There's a word for this, and it is vandalism. We must not vandalize the faith in the name of pragmatism!

In preaching the gospel, we are not hawking cheap wares; we are inviting people into a cathedral of astonishment. But  here is something I have noticed from my own experience in visiting some of the great cathedrals of the world—the interior has to be seen in person to be appreciated. Great Gothic cathedrals can have a beautiful exterior (though it is more often imposing), but their true beauty is found in the interior. These cathedrals are designed for the worshiper who enters the sanctuary, not for the casual passerby who only observes from outside. I've also noticed that it's virtually impossible to get a good representative photograph of the interior of a great cathedral. You can capture part of the cathedral in a photograph—this chapel or that transept—but you simply cannot capture what it is like to be surrounded by the vastness of a great Gothic cathedral from a photograph. It is simply too big to be captured from the perspective of a single vantage point—which is to say it cannot be explained; it can only be experienced. The only way to experience the astonishment of a vast cathedral is to enter the cathedral yourself. This is just the way it is with Christianity. There is some beauty that can be seen from without, though it may also seem a bit imposing. But to really experience the astonishing beauty of Christianity—the beauty that saves the world—you must enter the cathedral yourself. There is no explanation of Christianity that can adequately represent the experience of it. Again, Christianity is not something you possess; it is something you enter. It's not an explanation; it's a confession. And it's done by faith. We can witness to the astonishing beauty of Christianity, but to fully appreciate it, it must be experienced for one's self. So we will tell people of what we have found in this cathedral of astonishment called Christianity, but eventually we can say no more than "come and see."* And having said, "Come and see," let us make sure we take the seekers into the cathedral itself and not try to sell them a cheap replica.

In an essay on the Taj Mahal, Salman Rushdie eloquently makes the point that I am trying to communicate concerning astonishment and Christianity with my cathedral metaphor. Having been to Agra and the Taj Mahal a couple of times myself, I completely concur with what Salman Rushdie says, but more importantly, his essay is a perfect metaphor for what I'm trying to say about Christianity in the contemporary North American context.

> The problem with the Taj Mahal is that it has become so overlaid with accumulated meanings as to be almost impossible to see. When you arrive at the outer walls of the gardens in which the Taj is set, it's as if every hustler and hawker in Agra is waiting for you to make the familiarity-breeds-contempt problem worse, peddling imitation Mahals of every size and price. This leads to a certain amount of shoulder-shrugging disenchantment. Recently, a British friend

---

* Psalm 66:5; see also Isaiah 66:18; Matthew 28:6; John 1:39, 46; Revelation 6:7.

who was about to make his first visit to India told me that he had decided to leave the Taj off his itinerary because of its overexposure. If I urged him not to, it's because of my own vivid memory of pushing my way for the first time through the jostling crowd of imitation vendors, past all the myriad hawkers of meaning and interpretation, and into the presence of *the thing itself*, which utterly overwhelmed me, and made all my notions about its devaluation feel totally and completely redundant. The building itself left my skepticism in shreds. Announcing itself as itself, insisting with absolute force on its sovereign authority, it simply obliterated the million counterfeits of it and glowingly filled, once and forever, the place in the mind previously occupied by its simulacra.[6]

Wow! That's what I'm trying to say—not about the Taj Mahal, but about Christianity! Has contemporary Americanized Christianity become so overlaid with accumulated cultural assumptions that it is almost impossible to see? Have the evangelistic hustlers and hawkers produced a certain amount of shoulder-shrugging disenchantment concerning Christianity within our society? Have we peddled miniature imitation Christianities that people can "use" to the detriment of the mystery and beauty of the faith? I'm afraid it's all too true. So what is the solution? Exactly what Salman Rushdie says—to push through the jostling crowd of imitation-vendors, past all the myriad hawkers of meaning and interpretation, and into the presence of *the thing itself*. To rediscover Christianity in all of its astonishing mystery and beauty will utterly overwhelm us and make all of our notions about its devaluation feel completely redundant. It will leave our skepticism in shreds. If we can once again allow Christianity to announce itself as itself, it will simply obliterate the counterfeits and once again be a cathedral of astonishment!

The first human encounter with the epicenter of Christian faith—the empty tomb—left the recipients of that encounter trembling, astonished, and silent. It was Shock and Awe. Fear and Trembling. *Fear and Trembling* was the title Søren Kierkegaard gave to his most important book. Kierkegaard, more than anyone of his era, understood that to engage ourselves with God must involve an initial response of awe—or fear and trembling. It's *God* we're engaging with, after all! Of course Kierkegaard borrowed the "fear and trembling" phrase from the apostle Paul who, in writing to the church in Philippi, told the fledgling Christians to "work out your own salvation with fear and trembling."* But what does that mean? Work out our salvation? With fear and trembling? If we shrink salvation down to a ticket to heaven, Paul's exhortation makes little sense. But if we understand salvation as Maximus the Confessor described it—"an entirely new way to be human"— then it makes perfect sense. Salvation is not securing a seat for the bus to heaven, but a thorough living out of resurrection implications. Paul is telling the Philippian Christians that, regarding their salvation, they are to work it out, walk it out, live it out—and to do so with fear and trembling. Why fear and trembling? Because what we have involved ourselves with in Christ is so utterly astonishing!

Paul's exhortation to work out our salvation with fear and trembling begins with "therefore." Paul's "therefore" is placed immediately following a poem (thought to be a very early Christian hymn). The poem goes like this:

---

* Philippians 2:12

Who, though he was in the form of God,
did not regard equality with God
as something to be exploited,
but emptied himself,
taking the form of a slave,
being born in human likeness.

And being found in human form,
he humbled himself
and became obedient to the point of death—
even death on a cross.

Therefore God also highly exalted him
and gave him the name
that is above every name,
so that at the name of Jesus
every knee should bend,
in heaven and on earth and under the earth,
and every tongue should confess
that Jesus Christ is Lord,
to the glory of God the Father.

—Philippians 2:6–11

Therefore…Work it out! Walk it out! Live it out! What? Your own salvation! How? With fear and trembling! Shock and awe! Wonder and astonishment! Not because you have a morbid dread of the God revealed in Christ, but because everything about salvation is so astonishing! Think about it…God became human. Not just human, but a slave. He humbled himself. How far? All the way to death. Even death on a cross! And what happened? God exalted Jesus to his right hand. God made Jesus Lord of heaven and earth! This is the gospel. And this gospel properly heard and rightly received must first of all produce astonishment! Failure to be astonished by the gospel is proof that we are hearing the gospel only as a cliché—a cliché like a peddler's imitation of the Taj Mahal in Agra. Eugene Peterson describes the problem of salvation reduced to cliché like this:

> "Salvation" is the single word that most succinctly characterizes this play of Jesus in history. If the phrase had not long ago been reduced to cliché, "Jesus saves" would serve admirably as an adequate summary for what our Scriptures have to say on the subject. But bumper stickers and graffiti have isolated the phrase so completely from the story to which it is the punch line that all the meaning has been drained out of the words. We need to recover the salvation *story* if the salvation *words* are to mean anything. Salvation is not a one-night stand.[7]

Salvation is not a one-night stand. Salvation is not a ticket to heaven. Salvation is not a sinner's prayer prayed once upon a time. Salvation is what happens as the story of Jesus intersects and becomes enfolded into our own story. Salvation is what continues to happen as we live our lives out of the ongoing astonishment of the gospel story. "Jesus Saves" as an isolated slogan quickly degenerates into empty cliché utterly devoid of any capacity to astonish. It's salvation, not as a cathedral, but as a bumper sticker. It's salvation, not as symphony, but as sound bite. When the gospel is removed from its proper context of story and compressed into a slogan, it becomes commercialized and clichéd. Salvation as slogan or formula or principle is doomed to end up as a trite cliché that people easily dismiss. We must never forget that the gospel is first and foremost a *story*—a story that when properly told still has the capacity to astonish... and save.

I have one more thought regarding Christianity as a cathedral of astonishment. Cathedrals are not chapels. Cathedrals are vast and enormous. Chapels are small and subordinate. But cathedrals contain chapels. Cathedrals are enormous and beautiful edifices of worship constructed in the shape of the cruciform. Chapels are smaller places of worship with their own altar and dedication within a cathedral. It is not unusual for there to be many worship services happening simultaneously in various chapels within a single cathedral. This is how we need to understand the various branches and denominations within Christianity. Christianity is a vast and enormous cathedral built around the astonishing and seminal confession that Jesus is Lord. But most of us worship in particular chapels—whether Orthodox, Catholic, Anglican, Protestant, Evangelical, Pentecostal. This is not necessarily a bad thing, as long as we don't confuse the chapel for the cathedral. Unfortunately, confusing a particular chapel for the whole cathedral is all too common. Worse yet, some rigidly sectarian groups seem to have confused a janitor's closet for the whole cathedral!

One of the greatest discoveries I have made in my Christian journey is the discovery of the entire body of Christ—the whole vast cathedral of Christianity. For too long my own version of Christianity was narrow and shortsighted. Fortunately, by the grace of God, I eventually discovered that I needed the whole scope of the historical church and the whole scale of the ecumenical church. As I have learned to visit the various chapels contained within the great cathedral of Christianity, I have been able to avail myself of the riches particular to those chapels—Orthodox, Catholic, Anglican, Protestant, Evangelical, Pentecostal. Theologians like David Bentley Hart, Hans Urs von Balthasar, N. T. Wright, Stanley Hauerwas, Miroslav Volf,

Clark Pinnock—all hailing from different "chapels"—have
greatly enriched my Christianity with their brilliant work.
Whether it's Orthodox theology and art, Catholic appreciation for mystery, Anglican liturgy and prayer, Protestant
prominence of Scripture, Evangelical emphasis on conversion,
Pentecostal experience of the Holy Spirit—all of these "chapels"
have their particular treasures that have made Christianity for
me much more rich, beautiful, and astonishing.

## CHAPTER 7

# A SHELTER FROM
# THE STORM

OR THE CHURCH to recover its proper form of beauty, we need to employ the appropriate metaphors, for without the correct metaphors we will inevitably have a wrong idea about the shape of beauty and what we need to become. In an increasingly technocratic society awash in the unimaginative prose of technical language, we can forget the power of metaphor. Metaphors are important. There is a kind of magic in metaphor. Human beings have a natural genius for metaphor. Metaphors give us a concrete way of imagining and communicating what otherwise may remain purely abstract, and abstract ideas have a hard time taking root in our life.

A prophetic imagination is fueled by metaphors. The Old Testament prophets loved metaphors. Isaiah, Jeremiah, Ezekiel, and the rest of these Hebrew poets were masters at using metaphors in ways that flood our imagination with new ideas and visions for alternative futures. Isaiah gives us the image of a lion and a lamb lying down together, and it has become an iconic metaphor of peace. Jeremiah gives us a picture of Messiah as a branch growing up from the house of David and filling the earth with the fruit of righteousness. Ezekiel gives us the picture of a trickle of water flowing from a new kind of temple that turns into a river and heals the alkaline wastelands of the earth. These metaphors fill us with hope and help us see that the way of the broken world does not have to remain a dead end.

Jesus, the living incarnation of the Word of God, frequently gave incarnation to his identity by the use of metaphors. So Jesus speaks of himself as bread, water, light, a door, a vine, a road, a shepherd. John the Revelator wildly piles metaphor upon metaphor to communicate the triumph of the Lamb and to bring the Bible to its apocalyptic apex. Yes, metaphors are important. Without them our imagination remains unengaged and ideas evaporate into the ethereal mist of abstract theory. Metaphors are powerful. The wrong metaphor will give us the wrong idea and put us on the wrong road. The right metaphor unlocks our imagination to see mysteries in a new light and point us in the right direction. Much of the genius of the Bible is its skillful use of metaphors.

To understand the church we need the help of metaphors. If I say, "The church is God's alternative society formed around faith in Jesus Christ"—the statement is true enough, but it doesn't inspire the imagination. It's purely conceptual. So to aid our attempt to imagine and understand the church and its mission, we are given numerous prophetic metaphors in Scripture. The church is a body, a bride, a branch, a city, a temple, a vineyard, an army. These metaphors energize our imagination about the church. Of course, no one metaphor can communicate all that might be said or needs to be said about a subject as vast and rich as the church. So we have many ecclesial metaphors. But there are times when certain metaphors are more appropriate than others.

For a number of years now, some segments of the American church have been quite enthusiastic about the militaristic metaphor—they love the idea of being the army of the Lord. Not long ago I spoke in a church that had decked out their sanctuary with sandbags, machine guns, and even a faux tank in an over-the-top use of the military metaphor. I happened to be preaching on the Beatitudes. You can imagine the incongruence! Preaching "blessed are the peacemakers" while surrounded by the paraphernalia of combat was a surreal experience that provided moments of deep irony. But the military metaphor is popular. There is something about the psyche of some American evangelicals that makes them almost giddy about the military motif. Evangelist G.I. Joe! But there is something unhelpful about the military metaphor if it feeds an antagonistic "us versus them" attitude. I would like to suggest that in our current culture-war climate the militaristic metaphor may not be the best choice. Many outside the church misunderstand the metaphor and even feel threatened by it. For that matter, it might be best if churches hosted by superpowers forgo the military metaphor altogether. I know my Christian friends in Russia are uncomfortable with the military metaphor. It's too easy for the metaphor to be misunderstood (both by those inside and those outside the church). Besides, we are left with plenty of other options. Why not stress being the body of Christ, the bride of Christ, the city of God, the temple of the Lord, the vineyard of the Lord?

In summing up his Sermon on the Mount, Jesus gives three successive metaphors. First, Jesus talks about two roads.

One is wide and easy, but it leads to destruction. The other is narrow and hard, but it leads to life. Then Jesus speaks of two trees. One bears good fruit and lives on, while the other bears bad fruit and is cut down and burned. Finally, Jesus gives the metaphor of two houses. One is built on the rock so that it withstands the wind, rain, and flood; the other is built on the sand and collapses in the storm.* This final metaphor, which Jesus uses to conclude his masterpiece sermon, is particularly hopeful to those of us interested in reimagining the church in a beautiful way. It's the metaphor of a shelter from the storm.

But the metaphor itself is not original with Jesus. Jesus is borrowing it from Isaiah. Three times the poet Isaiah uses the "shelter from the storm" metaphor as he prophesies the coming of the Messianic age. First Isaiah speaks of Zion in the age of Messiah as a "shelter from the storm."† Then Isaiah speaks of God's care for the poor and needy as a "shelter from the storm."‡ Finally, Isaiah imagines a king who will reign in righteousness and rule in justice and whose kingdom will be a "shelter from the storm."§

Eight centuries after Isaiah, Jesus used Isaiah's metaphor to close his Sermon on the Mount. Jesus understood that he and his followers were ushering in the long-awaited kingdom of God and that in so doing they were building what Isaiah described as a shelter from the storm. And what a beautiful metaphor it is! In a world weary of 24/7 polarized rancor and angry "us versus them" rhetoric, the church as a shelter from the storm is a far more appealing metaphor than "storm

---

* Matthew 7:13–27
† Isaiah 4:2–6, esv
‡ Isaiah 25:1–5, esv
§ Isaiah 32:1–2, esv

troopers for Jesus." Most people are not going to find an invitation to church in the form of, "We're in a great battle; come fight on our side," very attractive. The last thing most people want in their lives is a more intense sense of conflict. But what if we allow a new metaphor to inspire our imagination in a new way? What if we frame our invitation for people to find their way into the church in terms of finding shelter from the storm? What if we understood our evangelistic task as inviting a bedraggled humanity beaten down by the cold rains of modern life into welcoming churches envisioned as a safe and warm shelter? Wouldn't that be beautiful?

A shelter from the storm is a beautiful metaphor that can help us be true to the form of beauty. And Isaiah wasn't the last poet to recognize the lyrical beauty of a shelter from the storm and its power to capture our imagination. In his mesmerizing song "Shelter From the Storm," Bob Dylan paints the picture of a woman who offers a worn-out wayfarer a particular kind of kindness. Here are five of the ten verses from the song:

> 'Twas in another lifetime, one of toil and blood
> When blackness was a virtue and the road was full
>      of mud
> I came in from the wilderness, a creature void of form
> "Come in," she said, "I'll give you shelter from the
>      storm."
>
> And if I pass this way again, you can rest assured
> I'll always do my best for her, on that I give my word.
> In a world of steel-eyed death, and men who are
>      fighting to be warm
> "Come in," she said, "I'll give you shelter from the
>      storm."

I was burned out from exhaustion, buried in the hail
Poisoned in the bushes an' blown out on the trail
Hunted like a crocodile, ravaged in the corn
"Come in," she said, "I'll give you shelter from the
    storm."

Suddenly I turned around and she was standin' there
With silver bracelets on her wrists and flowers in her
    hair.
She walked up to me so gracefully and took my
    crown of thorns
"Come in," she said, "I'll give you shelter from the
    storm."

I've heard newborn babies wailin' like a mournin' dove
And old men with broken teeth stranded without love.
Do I understand your question, man, is it hopeless
    and forlorn?
"Come in," she said, "I'll give you shelter from the
    storm."[1]

Every time I hear that song I can't help but ask, who is
this woman who offers shelter from the storm? And I always
answer—the church! The church is to be that beautiful bride
of Christ with silver bracelets on her wrist and flowers in her
hair offering shelter from the storm to creatures void of form,
to those burned out from exhaustion, to old men with broken
teeth stranded without love. Yes! In a world of steel-eyed
death and men who are fighting to be warm, it's the church
that offers shelter from the storm!

A shelter from the storm is a beautiful metaphor of the
church. It's not an angry church on a crusade for political
causes or a detached church disseminating dogma to a dis-
interested culture. Instead, try imagining a place where it's

always safe and warm—this is the church as a shelter from the storm. It's immensely appealing. And it's the very metaphor Jesus leaves lingering in our imagination as he concludes his Sermon on the Mount. In his summation Jesus tells us that if we will live his teaching, we will build a house on the rock-solid foundation that will stand when the rains fall, the winds blow, and the floods rise. To say it plainly, a church that lives the Sermon on the Mount will be a shelter from the storm.

The Sermon on the Mount is Jesus at the height of his homiletical powers; it is Jesus's greatest, most complete, and most important sermon. It's not an arbitrary collection of sayings or disassociated ideas. It is a sermon! It is a coherent sermon where one idea flows with divine logic into the next and the conclusion is related to the introduction, completing the circuit of this masterpiece sermon. Jesus begins his seminal sermon with an eightfold declaration concerning the nature of the kingdom of God and who it is who will be most blessed with its arrival. We call this octagonal announcement the Beatitudes (literally "the blessings"). Jesus announces these as blessed: the poor in spirit, the mourners, the meek, those hungering for justice, the merciful, the pure-hearted, the peacemakers, and the persecuted. The sermon that follows is an elaboration upon the kingdom of God as framed by the Beatitudes. Finally Jesus closes his sermon with the shelter from the storm metaphor. So let's put it all together—the shelter from the storm is the house built on the Beatitudes.

It should also be remembered that Jesus said the house not built on obedience to his words would fall. This was not just a bit of timeless truth but also a prophecy with a historic fulfillment. Jesus was pronouncing judgment on the corrupt temple, which, though it clung to a form of godliness, had departed from the ethics of mercy and justice—ethics that belong inherently to the kingdom of God and that were always intended to define covenantal identity. And what happened? Within a generation of Jesus's ministry the temple in Jerusalem was swept away by a military siege that was a storm of cataclysmic proportions. "And great was its fall!"[*]

The destruction of Jerusalem and the Jewish temple in A.D. 70 (forty years after the death and resurrection of Jesus) was hugely significant. Jesus had repeatedly warned that if Israel continued in their hell-bent ways of envisioning the kingdom of God in nationalistic terms and coming through violent revolution, the results would be disastrous. And so it was. Tragically, all Jesus had foretold concerning Jerusalem came to pass. Along with his resurrection, the other primary vindication of Jesus's life and teaching was the fulfillment of his numerous predictions that, because Jerusalem had rejected the peaceful ways of Messiah, the city and its temple would be destroyed.[†]

Jesus's vision was the establishment of a new kind of kingdom and the construction of a new kind of temple. This vision was to be carried out through what Jesus was building— "On this rock I will build my church."[‡] So despite the fact that in A.D. 70 Herod's temple came to an end, the new temple that Jesus was and is constructing continues to endure. This temple is "built upon the foundation of the apostles and prophets, with Christ Jesus himself as the cornerstone."[§] Wherever the church seriously seeks to live according to the way of Christ,

---

[*]   Matthew 7:27
[†]   See Luke 19:41–44; 21:20–24; 23:27–31.
[‡]   Matthew 16:18
[§]   Ephesians 2:20

there is found a shelter from the storm. So if we understand the Beatitudes as the foundation of Jesus's teaching (the rock), and we want our churches to be a shelter from the storm, we are going to have to get serious about adopting the beautiful form of the Beatitudes. An aesthetic Christianity expressing the beauty that saves the world will excel in these eight things:

- Welcoming the poor in spirit
- Comforting those who mourn
- Esteeming the meek
- Hungering for justice
- Extending mercy
- Having a pure heart
- Being peacemakers
- Enduring persecution

Let's consider the eight announcements of the Beatitudes that make up the octagonal foundation that we are to build upon. It is first of all vital we understand that the Beatitudes are not platitudes. They are not commonsense sayings. They are the very opposite. The Beatitudes are often paradoxes and deeply counterintuitive. The Beatitudes are subversive to the established order—they are the subversive values of the kingdom of God. The Beatitudes are the counterintuitive wisdom of God that turns the assumed values of a superpower culture on its head. The Beatitudes are the antithetical ethos to the superpower mantra of "we're number one!" The Beatitudes are deliberately designed to shock us. If we're not shocked by the Beatitudes, it's only because we have tamed them with a patronizing sentimentality—and being sentimental about Jesus is the religious way of *ignoring* Jesus! Too often the Beatitudes are set aside into the category of "nice things that Jesus said that I don't really understand."

The Beatitudes do not reveal their full meaning at first glance. They do not yield their treasures to the casual enquirer. They require thought, reflection, and meditation. The wisdom of the Beatitudes will only dawn on us slowly. We have much to learn and just as much to unlearn. Every serious Jesus follower should memorize the Beatitudes. This is our manifesto, our Magna Carta, our Bill of Rights. But despite their obvious significance, the Beatitudes remain foreign to us. We have not been formed by the values of the Beatitudes; we have been raised on the received text of a superpower. (The notion that the received text of a superpower and the sacred text of the Sermon on the Mount can be made to fit together nicely is lunacy!) Contemporary Americans are scripted in a way that is completely counter to the values of the Beatitudes. We certainly *don't* bless poverty or sorrow or meekness or hunger or persecution—yet it is the poor and sorrowful and meek and hungry and persecuted that we find Jesus blessing in the Beatitudes. At the very least, this should perplex us.

It's also helpful to understand that the Beatitudes are not advice or instructions or qualifications. They are nothing like that. They are not dictates or laws; the Beatitudes are *announcements*. Jesus is proclaiming the arrival of the kingdom of God, and with the Beatitudes Jesus is announcing who it is who is going to be most blessed with its arrival. Jesus is telling us in whose ears the gospel of the kingdom is going to really sound like good news. It is an unsettling fact that the inauguration of the kingdom of God brings a radical change to the accepted order of how the world has always been run. The Beatitudes announce that change. This is why Jesus says things like, "The last will be first, and the first will be last."* It is at this point that those accustomed to confessing they are "number one" should begin to squirm.

What Jesus is announcing in the Beatitudes is a radical reordering of assumed values; some will hear it as good news, while others will be threatened by it. Those for whom the long-established order has been advantageous—the winners in the game, the top dogs—are not really looking for things to change; they have a vested interest in the status quo. This is going to place Jesus at odds with the power brokers of the age— then and now. After all, it wasn't the poor and marginalized who conspired to crucify Jesus; it was Caiaphas and Herod and Pilate—those who had a powerful stake in the present arrangement. But for the losers in the game—those scraping the bottom of life's barrel, the marginalized and forgotten, the left out—what Jesus announces is indeed good news.

---

Blessed are the poor in spirit, for theirs is the kingdom of heaven.
                                        —MATTHEW 5:3

*Blessed are those who are poor at being spiritual,*
*For the kingdom of heaven is well-suited for ordinary*
    *people.*

Though I would not claim this is the only way to under-stand the first beatitude, I think we can understand part of

---

*   Matthew 20:16

what Jesus is saying as something like this: "Hey, all of you who are not very good at being spiritual, today is your lucky day, because the kingdom of God is for you too. So come on in!" For people who are poor at being spiritual (which is most people), this announcement really is good news. But do you see how counterintuitive this is? The kingdom of God is coming on earth, and who would we think would be the first ones invited in? The religious. The devout. The observant. The ones rich in spirituality. The ones good at being spiritual. But that's not how Jesus issued the invitation, and it's not what happened. It was the spiritual elites, the Pharisees, Sadducees, priests, scribes, and Torah lawyers who had the most trouble with Jesus. The company of Jesus's followers was largely comprised of people for whom being spiritual was not their primary identity—fishermen, tradesmen, tax collectors, and a wide variety of sinners.

This goes a long way in explaining why Jesus wasn't very popular with the spiritual experts and religious professionals. To them it seemed like Jesus was lowering the standard so that *anyone* could get in on what God was doing. Jesus seemed to be announcing that the favor of God was now indiscriminate. And for those who had made a long practice of being spiritual, it didn't seem fair to let just anyone in on it. But we will remember that Jesus gave several parables to confirm their suspicions that these Johnny-come-lately penitents would be just as welcome and equally rewarded as those who were longtime experts at being spiritual.* It is clear this was Jesus's attitude and practice. The question is, "Do *you* think this is good news?" If not, it's probably because you are rich in spiritual

---

* See Matthew 20:1–16.

things, which is fine; it's just that Jesus is not announcing anything in particular to you in the first beatitude. Blessed are the *poor* in spirit.

Every culture has those for whom being spiritual comes natural. They are the ones who form some kind of priestly class. These are the ones who don't mind being called upon to pray in public. Public prayer belongs to their skill set. They are rich in spirituality. There is certainly nothing wrong with this, but it's a minority of people who are naturally gifted at being spiritual. What about you? If you are the one who is regularly called upon to offer a prayer at the family reunion picnic, you can be pretty sure you are rich at being spiritual. But for most people, being called upon to pray in public is almost terrifying. It's to them that Jesus announces good news: "Blessed are you who are poor at being spiritual; you can be a part of this too." Jesus isn't telling you *to be* poor at being spiritual (Jesus isn't telling you to be anything!); Jesus is simply making an announcement of good news to ordinary people who are poor at being spiritual and have always felt like they were outsiders in the things of God.

For our churches to be shelters from the storm, which ordinary people find welcoming, we must get rid of an "elite forces" mentality. There are churches that intentionally fashion themselves as "special forces" and "super spiritual." They are Green Berets for Jesus. They can pray longer, sing louder, worship better, fast more frequently, and be more "on fire" than any church in town. They know this, and they are quite proud of it. And as far as it goes, it can be rather impressive. They are a kind of venue for spiritual Olympians where great feats of extreme spirituality are on display. For them spirituality is a kind of competition based on comparison. But here's the thing: although people may indeed be impressed by it all, the average person will never feel welcome in that kind of church. They're just not that good at being spiritual. It is to these ordinary people that Jesus is making his announcement of good news. And believe me, the poor in spirit hear it as good news! When I preached this first beatitude as good news for those who are poor at being spiritual in my own church, I had a huge response. For weeks afterward people would come up to me, often with tears in their eyes, and tell me how liberated they felt after hearing that Jesus pronounced a blessing on those who are poor at being spiritual. I had preached the gospel, and the poor in spirit had heard it as good news.

It's true that the gospel of Luke records Jesus as saying, "Blessed are you who are poor"—period.* In Luke's Beatitudes, Jesus simply blesses the poor, and the further categorization of "in spirit" is omitted. In Luke, Jesus blesses the poor without reference to what kind of poverty it is. The truth is this: Jesus meets us at our point of poverty, not our place of strength. If we want to position ourselves to receive Christ's blessing, we must identify an area of need and cry out for grace from there. If we think we have no area of weakness, need, or poverty, we essentially have no need for Jesus. This is why in the Book of Revelation Jesus condemns the people in the church of Laodicea for arrogantly confessing, "I am rich, I have prospered, and I need nothing." They were essentially saying, "Thank you very much, Jesus, but I really don't need you right now because I'm not poor." So be it. Jesus has no blessing for them. The grace of Christ is perfected in weakness and poverty, not in strength and wealth.† As Mary said of Messiah in

---

* Luke 6:20
† See 2 Corinthians 12:9.

her prophetic *Magnificat*, "He has filled the hungry with good things but has sent the rich away empty."* This is the spirit of the first beatitude—and to the poor it is beautiful.

---

Blessed are those who mourn, for they will be comforted.
—MATTHEW 5:4

*Blessed are the depressed who mourn and grieve,*
*For they create space to encounter comfort from another.*

The paradoxical nature of the Beatitudes is on particular display here. Jesus is essentially saying, "Blessed and happy are those who mourn and aren't blessed and happy." A paradox indeed, but the wisdom of God is found, not in "solving" the paradox, but in entering its mystery. As with the first beatitude, this is not an instruction but an announcement. Jesus is not so much telling us to mourn as he is making an announcement to those who do mourn. Sorrow is a necessary consequence of loving others and being fully engaged with humanity. If our plan is to go through life minimizing pain and avoiding as much sorrow as possible, we will do so as a shallow people, and Jesus has nothing to announce to us in the second beatitude—he simply leaves us in our prosaic self-contentment. It is through the work of grief that we carve depth into our souls and create space to be filled with comfort from another.

In this way, grief is understood, not as a reality to be denied, but as a work to be attended to. In a simple-minded, paper-thin, pseudo-Christian culture where banal happiness seems to be the highest goal, we don't want to attend to the work of

---

* Luke 1:53, NIV

grief; we put it off as an unpleasant task or something beneath our station. But this has consequences. In refusing to attend to the work of grief, our soul becomes a vast, bleak, featureless wasteland—a kind of barren salt flat where nothing grows. In such a state the soul can never know true comfort and joy; it can only be anesthetized with entertainment. It is in the work of grief that space and depth are created—space and depth that can be filled with something other than an entertainment-induced coma of self-contentment.

When we are self-content, we tend not to look beyond ourselves; we don't feel the need to do so. (Or is it that we simply don't feel at all?) In the state of self-contentment we have no affinity with suffering. It's foreign to us; we don't understand it. If we remain a stranger to sorrow, it is virtually impossible to have compassion (compassion means "shared pain"). Here in the second beatitude, Jesus is making an important announcement to those who, instead of finding a means of avoiding personal pain and shared sorrow, have allowed themselves to be sculpted by pain and sorrow. Jesus seems to be saying that it is those who have given up being comfortably numb through shallow contentment and have instead engaged in the real work of grief—for there is much in this world to grieve over—who are the ones who will encounter the deep comfort of the kingdom of God.

Yet it is at just this point that we encounter a problem. As a superpower culture, we feel we are somehow exempt from sorrow and mourning. We have the biggest economy and the best military. We're rich, and we win our wars. After all, our nation was founded partly on the idea that the pursuit of happiness is an inalienable right. How can we mourn? Why would we? No doubt we have taken the right to pursue happiness quite seriously; some would say we are running ourselves to exhaustion in the pursuit of it! So when it comes to sorrow and grief, America has long cultivated a culture of denial. It's all part of the baggage of a superpower that has as its unofficial motto, "We're number one!" John the Revelator understood that all empires see themselves as immune to sorrow and mocked this delusion when he depicted Rome as boasting, "I sit as a queen; I am not a widow, and I will never mourn."*

As a superpower nation and a happiness-obsessed culture, we whistle past the graveyard, imagining we will never mourn and pretending we don't know that death is the backdrop of human existence. Perhaps like no other people in history we strive to ignore our pain and deny our sorrow—we have become a people addicted to entertainment and schooled in denial. None of this is healthy. Our practice is a frightened response to the possibility of pain—we don't think we can bear it, so we pretend we don't know about it. American culture, having been schooled in the denial mechanism that is part and parcel of a superpower, doesn't know how to mourn. This is problematic. That the American church, taking its cues from the wider culture, doesn't know how to grieve and lament is an absolute tragedy. American evangelicalism, especially in some of the more "success in life" oriented forms, has cultivated a cheap, shallow, happy-clappy, Disney-esque culture that refuses to recognize that grief and lamentation are part of the necessary work that belongs to the people of God.

Much of our determined effort to erect an artificial façade of happiness stems from the misguided idea that somehow it is our Christian "duty" to be happy all the time—as if we

---

* Revelation 18:7, NIV

have to prove the validity of the gospel by maintaining a constant saccharine joviality *à la* the cartoon caricature that is Ned Flanders in *The Simpsons.* The time-honored symbol of the Christian faith is the cruciform—a symbol of co-suffering love and sacrificial death transformed by faith in the resurrection. (I wonder if one of the reasons Protestants have been nervous about crucifixes is that it makes the reality of suffering too apparent?) I sometimes think we are trying to replace the symbol of the cross with a smiley face! Serious Christianity has given way to "inspirational" Christianity, which is turning into insipid Christianity. Have we replaced a serious theology of the cross with a pop psychology of happiness? Have we traded something sublime and serious, majestic and mysterious, for something silly, prosaic, and shallow—a juvenile obsession with cheap happiness? I don't think I'm overstating the problem.

Because we are uncomfortable with sorrow, we passively enforce a kind of mandated happiness in our churches. Instead of weeping with those who weep, we want everybody to just cheer up. And we want them to cheer up *for our sake*...because we are so terribly uncomfortable with their sorrow. What we should do instead is join them in their sorrow and assist them in the work of grief. When human beings suffer tragedy and profound loss, there is a certain amount of grieving that is required. But in the deep mystery of human inner-connectivity, the work of grieving does not have to be done alone. When we choose to bear the burden of sorrow with others, it really does lighten the load for the suffering. The question is, can we create churches that understand that mourning is not a sign of weakness, but a spiritual work to be attended to—a spiritual work that Jesus says leads to the blessedness of comfort from outside ourselves?

That lamentation is a spiritual practice clearly endorsed in Scripture should be obvious to anyone who has ever read the Psalms. The Psalms are filled with complaint, lamentation, and the outpouring of sorrow. David and the rest of the psalmists composed a surprising number of laments. Praying these laments will, over time, deepen our capacity for both mourning and comfort. Too often we approach the prayers in the Psalms by thumbing through them and looking for the one that expresses what we feel. But the point of praying the Psalms is not to express what we feel, but to feel what they express. If we take an individualistic and self-centered approach to the Psalms, we remain a shallow, self-obsessed people. But when we approach the Psalms with the understanding that we are part of a praying community and that to represent human sorrow before the throne of God is a holy task (no matter how we happen to feel that day), we deepen the capacity of our soul to receive divine comfort.

Then there is the sometimes surprising fact that there is a book in the Bible called *Lamentations*! There is an important truth to learn from this often overlooked book. In the historic chronology, Lamentations fits between Isaiah chapters 39 and 40 (Isaiah chapters 1–39 were written before the destruction of Jerusalem and the Babylonian exile; Isaiah chapters 40–66 were written during the exile). In Lamentations (presumably written by Jeremiah), the grieving prophet says repeatedly there is "none to comfort...none to comfort...none to comfort."* This is the work of grief. This is the lament of loss. And

---

* Lamentations 1:2, 17, 21, esv

it is this mourning that creates room for comfort. We see this when Isaiah chapter 40 (written after Lamentations) opens with these words: "Comfort, O comfort my people, says your God."[*] Lamentation had created space to receive comfort, and in due season comfort came in the form of Isaiah's prophecy of hope. This is the principle of Jesus's second beatitude: "Blessed are those who mourn, for they will be comforted."[†] If we can allow space in our churches for those who are mourning, without pressuring them to "get over it" and "cheer up," we will have created space for them to, in due time, encounter the comfort of hope that comes from the kingdom of God. This is part of being a shelter from the storm.

---

Blessed are the meek, for they will inherit the earth.
—MATTHEW 5:5

*Blessed are the quiet and content, the humble and unassuming, the gentle and trusting who are not grasping and clutching, for God will personally guarantee their share when heaven and earth become one.*

Matthew tells us that the multitude that formed the audience for Jesus's Sermon on the Mount was a mixed multitude coming from different places and representing diverse ethnic, religious, and political backgrounds.[‡] There were religious Jews from Judea with their devout commitment to Torah observance and keeping kosher. There were Galilean Jews for whom synagogue life, though important, was not the obsession it was

---

[*]   Isaiah 40:1
[†]   Matthew 5:4
[‡]   Matthew 4:25

for the Judeans. There were nonobservant Jews who, having dropped out of religious life altogether, were dubbed "sinners." There were Greeks from the Decapolis region with their sophisticated love of art, philosophy, and athletics. And of course there were the Romans—the triumphant foreign occupiers from the dominant superpower. What Jesus has to say in the Beatitudes and the Sermon on the Mount he addresses to *all* of these people. His sermon is not instructions on how to be religious or how to be Jewish (or Christian); Jesus's instructions are on how to be *human*. Jesus is revealing to the human race the narrow way that leads to life. Jesus is teaching us the counterintuitive way of God that makes life livable.

Perhaps the most counterintuitive of all the Beatitudes is the third blessing Jesus bestows. Jesus blesses the meek—the quiet, the gentle, the nonassertive, the nonaggressive—saying *they* will inherit the earth. But I doubt we believe this. We would say something different. Something like: "Blessed are the meek, for even though he comes in last, he'll be called a nice guy, receive a certificate of participation, and be named 'Miss Congeniality.'" That's what *we* think about the meek—but it's not what Jesus says! Jesus says the meek will *inherit the earth*. Inherit the earth?! Really?

That is the question, isn't it? Who gets the earth? Who gets to carve up the pie? Who gets the biggest and best piece? When the Roman soldiers stationed in Tiberius and standing on the edge of the crowd heard this pronouncement, they must have looked at each other with knowing smirks. They knew better. They knew how the real world was run. Rome ruled the world—from Britain to India. Caesar had conquered the world, and it was the Roman Empire that inherited the earth. You can be sure Rome didn't gain the world by being meek! Rome ruled the world because they were smart, bold, aggressive, and willing to make war to secure their superpower status. Yet here is this poor Galilean rabbi announcing that the meek will inherit the earth. Crazy talk. I'm sure the Roman soldiers had a good laugh.

Yet Jesus says it. The meek—the peaceable and nonaggressive—will inherit the earth. In fact, Jesus was saying nothing new. Psalm 37 says the meek are blessed and will inherit the earth.* Obviously Jesus is reminding his Jewish listeners that there is an alternative way of viewing the world other than seeing it through the lens of a self-aggrandizing superpower where it's dog-eat-dog, winner-take-all. Instead of grasping and clutching, there is the way of relaxing and trusting. This is why the thirty-seventh psalm opens with an exhortation to trust in God.

> Do not fret because of the wicked;
>   do not be envious of wrongdoers,
> for they will soon fade like the grass,
>   and wither like the green herb.
> Trust in the LORD, and do good;
>   so you will live in the land, and enjoy security.
> Take delight in the LORD,
>   and he will give you the desires of your heart.
> Commit your way to the LORD;
>   trust in him, and he will act.
> He will make your vindication shine like the light,
>   and the justice of your cause like the noonday.
> Be still before the LORD, and wait patiently for him;
>   do not fret over those who prosper in their way;
>   over those who carry out evil devices.
>
> —PSALM 37:1–7

---

* Psalm 37:11, 22, 29

There is a besetting paranoia that plagues the superpower ✕ mentality, and it most often manifests in an anxious obsession with security. Anxiety over security is the price the aggressive pay for clawing their way to the top—they are fated to live in constant dread that someone will take away their position of privilege. They worry about who might be hot on their heels. But Jesus, endorsing the psalmist, says there is another way, a way that is blessed and peaceful—the way of radical trust. The meek are not the driven, self-assertive, hyper-aggressive, grab-my-piece-of-the-pie people—they are not the winners and go-getters, the movers and shakers, the large and in charge. The meek are the ones who believe in God and are willing to trust God for their portion and their security. The way of violence and aggression is the way of Caesar. The way of meekness and trust is the way of Christ. And they are in contradiction to one another.

In the third beatitude, Jesus is endorsing the radical trust of the thirty-seventh psalm. The entire psalm can be read as a treatise on security for the people of God. The psalm advocates trusting the living God for security instead of relying upon the conventional means of force employed by the wicked. The psalm concludes with this promise:

> The salvation of the righteous is from the LORD;
>   he is their refuge in time of trouble.
> The LORD helps them and rescues them;
>   he rescues them from the wicked, and saves them,
>   because they take refuge in him.
>
> —PSALM 37:39–40

Of course I know what the "practical men of reason" will say: "If we don't aggressively guarantee our security by force, the wicked will certainly triumph and we will be dispossessed." But I also know what Jesus said: "Blessed are the meek, for they will inherit the earth." (You will have to choose whom you will believe. I'm sure the Romans thought it was crazy too.) The earth is *seized* by the aggressive and violent, but it is *inherited* by the meek and gentle. Inheritance is a family word, a relationship word, a grace word. Seizing is the way of Satan. Inheriting is the way of God.

It's probably unfortunate that in English "meek" rhymes with "weak." Too often we end up thinking they are synonyms. They are not. The meek are not weak. The meek are those who possess the strength of faith. The trusting meek believe they have a Father in heaven who oversees the affairs of men and who will personally guarantee their portion in the earth. Jesus was meek, but he certainly wasn't weak. The word *meek* (*praÿs* in the Greek) is only used three times in the Gospels—but each use is important. In the third beatitude, Jesus blessed the meek. Later Jesus describes himself as meek as he invites the weary to come to him and find rest.* Finally, the word *meek* is used in describing Jesus as he entered Jerusalem during his triumphal entry. Matthew quotes from Zechariah's prophecy:

> Tell the daughter of Zion,
> Look, your king is coming to you,
> humble [*praÿs*], and mounted on a donkey,
> and on a colt, the foal of a donkey.
>
> —MATTHEW 21:5

Matthew is saying that when Jesus entered Jerusalem riding a donkey (instead of a warhorse), he was fulfilling Zechariah's prophecy concerning how Messiah would come to Israel:

---

* Matthew 11:29

Rejoice greatly, O daughter Zion!
　Shout aloud, O daughter Jerusalem!
Lo, your king comes to you;
　triumphant and victorious is he,
humble and riding on a donkey,
　on a colt, the foal of a donkey.
He will cut off the chariot from Ephraim
　and the war-horse from Jerusalem;
and the battle bow shall be cut off,
　and he shall command peace to the nations;
his dominion shall be from sea to sea,
　and from the River to the ends of the earth.

　　　　　　　　　—ZECHARIAH 9:9–10

When Pilate rode into Jerusalem to take up residence in the
Antonia Fortress during the Passover, he rode on a warhorse
surrounded by soldiers. When Jesus rode into Jerusalem at
Passover, he rode on a donkey in a deliberate act of meekness
and as a prophetic rejection of the militaristic means of empire.
Of course by the time the week was over, Jesus had been crucified by Pilate. But whom did God vindicate? Whose empire
endures? Whose empire now stretches from sea to sea and to
the ends of the earth? The empire of Rome, which maintained
its security by its military, has been swept into the dustbin of
history, while the kingdom of Christ endures! How can this
be? The meek inherit the earth. This too is beautiful.

－－－－－－

Blessed are those who hunger and thirst for righteousness, for they shall be satisfied.

　　　　　　　　　—MATTHEW 5:6, ESV

*Blessed are those who ache for the world to be made right,*
*For them the government of God is a dream come true.*

The Beatitudes pose a direct challenge to the way the world is run. The Beatitudes are a subversive manifesto at odds with superpower agendas. As a result, the Beatitudes (when liberated from sentimental patronizing) elicit differing responses depending on who the hearer is. There are those who are blessed by the Beatitudes and hear them as a clarion call for welcome change. Others feel threatened by the radical revolution the Beatitudes appear to embody. Those who tend to feel the most threatened by the Beatitudes are those for whom the present arrangement is most advantageous. In other words, if you are a citizen of a modern-day superpower and generally like the way the world is arranged, you're probably going to initially feel more challenged than blessed by the Beatitudes. (But keep in mind that Jesus is trying to save you from the way of death!)

One of the problems with understanding the fourth beatitude is a peculiarity of the English language. Most languages (including the Greek of the New Testament) do not have separate words for righteousness and justice; rather, both concepts are contained in the same word. So when Jesus says, "Blessed are those who hunger and thirst for righteousness," he is also saying, "Blessed are those who hunger and thirst for justice." The Greek word *dikaiosyne* means both righteousness and justice. Unfortunately it is far more often translated as righteousness than justice. There is a problem with this. It allows us to shrink God's comprehensive justice to the realm of individual spirituality and private piety. We tend to think of righteousness as having to do with our personal relationship with God, whereas justice has to do with setting things right in the wider world. Of course God is interested in both. But by translating *dikaiosyne* almost exclusively as righteousness and almost never as justice, we pry apart the two concepts and gain the mistaken idea that God is interested in our spiritual condition but not our social arrangements.

This is a mistake, and the American evangelical church has suffered much from this mistake. As a result of a language peculiarity and the propensity to translate *dikaiosyne* almost exclusively as righteousness, we end up hearing the fourth beatitude as something like this: "Blessed are those who really want to be spiritual, for they shall be really spiritual." But that is *not* what Jesus is saying! Jesus is saying something more like this: "Blessed are those who ache for the world to be made right, for they shall be satisfied." Why? Because the kingdom (government) that Jesus is bringing into the world through his lordship has the agenda of reordering society according to God's justice. In this beatitude, Jesus isn't talking about private spirituality as much as he is talking about social justice. Of course the two go together. A person in right relationship with God is intensely interested in setting things right in the wider world.

The fourth beatitude is a very political beatitude. (Yes, let's talk about politics!) It's a misnomer (or even propaganda) to assert that Jesus wasn't political. The kingdom Jesus proclaimed had profound political consequences. Jesus challenged both the politics of Caesar and Herod. Jesus challenged the politics of Roman imperialism and the politics of Jewish nationalism. He did so with his own politics—the politics of love, which define the kingdom of God. To think somehow that Jesus was not political is to ignore the fact that Jesus was executed by the state for political reasons. (What Jesus was not was an adherent of any of the existing political movements.)

The kingdom of God is nothing less than God's alternative government, or, put simply, God's politics. And what are the politics of Jesus? The answer is obvious: the Sermon on the Mount. In his great sermon Jesus is giving humanity a new way of structuring society. But the Sermon on the Mount is not very much like the politics we are used to (conservative or liberal). And let's be clear about this—the politics of Jesus cannot be neatly summed up in the contemporary partisan categories of "right" or "left." Neither traditional conservatism nor progressive liberalism adequately represents the politics of Jesus (though both want to claim Jesus's endorsement). The politics of Jesus are neither right nor left, but transcendent, and Jesus's politics present a challenge to both liberals and conservatives. For example: If your liberal politics prevent you from defending the rights of the unborn and the sanctity of the family, you do not share the politics of Jesus. Likewise, if your conservative politics prevent you from defending the rights of the poor and immigrant, you do not share the politics of Jesus. Jesus is pro-life and pro-family; he is pro-poor and pro-immigrant. (But he's not running for office, because he *is* Lord!)

The prophet Malachi presented the coming of Messiah as a prophetic indictment of idolatry, immorality, and injustice.

> Yes, I'm on my way to visit you with Judgment. I'll present compelling evidence against sorcerers, adulterers, liars, those who exploit workers, those who take advantage of widows and orphans, those who are inhospitable to the homeless.
>
> —MALACHI 3:5, THE MESSAGE

Messiah has something to say about wrong spirituality (sorcery), wrong sexuality (adultery), and wrong ethics (perjury). But Messiah also has something to say about minimum wages, social welfare, and immigration reform. In other words, Messiah judges both personal righteousness and social justice. We cannot pit one against the other. We cannot choose either the "Personal Righteousness Jesus" or the "Social Justice Jesus"—the *real* Jesus is both!

As we listen to the Sermon on the Mount as modern Americans, we need to understand who we are in context. We are not the Galilean peasants who live in the shadow of the mighty superpower of Rome. We may want to romantically fancy ourselves as such, but we are not. We are the Romans with their status and privilege and for whom the present arrangement is very advantageous. So what should we do? Sit around and feel guilty about our privilege? No. Prosperity in and of itself is not a bad thing, and much of it is legitimately attributable to commendable virtues. But at the very least we should ache over what is wrong—the brokenness and inherent injustice of our world—and we should break free from the prosaic delusion that everything is okay. As we look at the world on a global scale, everything is far from okay. There is much injustice for the righteous to ache over. Consider the following facts—

- Sixteen percent of the world lives on less than one dollar per day.[2]

- Forty percent of the world lives on less than two dollars per day.[3]

- Eighty percent of the world lives on less than ten dollars per day.[4]

- Seventeen thousand children die from hunger every day.[5]

- The nations of the world spend three billion dollars per day on defense (56 percent by the United States).[6]

To put it in perspective: Each day, for every child who dies of hunger, the nations of the world spend $176,000 on security (which means defending themselves from one another). One hundred seventy-six thousand dollars per dead child on defense?! Do we really not see the madness and the injustice of this?! But we tell ourselves it's just the way things have to be. If we don't build billion-dollar bombers, things will go wrong—as if something has not already gone very, very wrong! So while the nations spend billions *every day* on their security...the orphans die and the widows weep. The very least the righteous can do is to ache over this and yearn for a better way. Hopefully the righteous can do much more than ache and yearn, but any step toward building a better world begins with a painful acknowledgment that the present arrangement is unacceptable.

In the fourth beatitude Jesus blesses those who ache over the pervasive injustice and deep brokenness of our world— Jesus blesses those who refuse to keep looking at the world through the rose-colored glasses of self-delusion. The people formed by the fourth beatitude will not submit to the despotic tyranny of the status quo—they ache for something better. Something better is what the kingdom of God brings, and it's why the disciples of Jesus pray day by day: "Thy government come, thy policy be done, on earth as it is in heaven." At the very least the disciples of Jesus formed by the fourth beatitude refuse to let the Beast have their imagination, and they will not perpetuate the satanic lie that "it has to be this way." No! It does *not* have to be this way! There *is* a better way! Jesus shows us that better way! Blessed are those who hunger and thirst for things to be made right, for they shall find immense satisfaction when and where the kingdom of Christ brings saving transformation and redemptive justice into the world. The disciples formed by the fourth beatitude know the difference between the intransient ugliness of injustice and the redeeming beauty of justice, and they long for the beauty of Christ's justice to save the world.

---

Blessed are the merciful, for they will receive mercy.
—MATTHEW 5:7

*Blessed are those who give mercy,*
*For they will get it back when they need it most.*

The Beatitudes are a window into the interior life of Jesus Christ, and they reveal to us his beautiful personality. If we ask, "What is Jesus like?," we can give no better answer than to say Jesus is like the Beatitudes. The Beatitudes uniquely capture the content of Christ's character. Jesus is drawn to the poor and sorrowful, and he stands up for the meek and persecuted. Jesus exhibits justice and mercy, and he endorses purity and peacemaking. This is what Jesus is like. If we attempt to understand Jesus apart from the Beatitudes, we inevitably get

Jesus wrong. Getting Jesus right is absolutely essential if we are to recover the beauty of Christianity, because Jesus *is* the beauty of Christianity! To see Jesus as he is, is to see the infinite beauty of God expressed in a human life.

At the close of the poetic prologue to his Gospel, the apostle John makes a shocking statement when he says, "No one has ever seen God."* Why is this shocking? It's shocking because the Hebrew Scriptures are full of accounts of those who have seen God. For example:

- Abraham saw God and shared a meal with him—Genesis 18:1–33.

- Jacob saw God at the top of the ladder in Bethel—Genesis 28:10–22.

- Moses saw God face-to-face in the tent of meeting—Exodus 33:11.

- The seventy elders of Israel saw God on Mount Sinai—Exodus 24:11.

- Isaiah saw God in the year King Uzziah died— Isaiah 6:1–13.

- Ezekiel saw God in his glory by the river Chebar—Ezekiel 1:1–28.

Don't think for a moment that John was not aware of each and every one of these stories. Of course he knew about these scriptural accounts of people who had seen God. So why is John contradicting the Old Testament? Because John wants to shock us. Why? Because John wants to show us Jesus, and

---

* John 1:18

everything about Jesus is shocking. John is not afraid to contradict the sacred and inspired Hebrew Scriptures because Jesus dared to contradict the sacred and inspired Hebrew Scriptures! Jesus did this repeatedly in the Sermon on the Mount.

> You have heard that it said, "An eye for an eye and a tooth for a tooth." But I say to you, Do not resist an evildoer. But if anyone strikes you on the right cheek, turn the other also.
>
> —MATTHEW 5:38–39

This is just one example of where Jesus clearly contradicts the Torah. In his famous dictum to turn the other cheek, Jesus countermands the scriptural law of justice as equivalent retribution, and he does so *by his own authority.* "You have heard it said…but *I* say to you." This is shocking. It's why the Jewish rabbi Jacob Neusner, though an admirer of Jesus, ultimately rejects what Jesus calls for in the Sermon on the Mount, because as Neusner says, "Only God can demand what Jesus asks of me."[7] Rabbi Neusner doesn't believe Jesus has the authority to countermand the Torah because only God has that authority. Precisely. So the apostle John is saying something very bold, because what Jesus claimed about himself was very bold. In saying, "No one has ever seen God," John is not saying the Old Testament accounts of people seeing God were fabrications; he is simply saying that no matter what visions, revelations, epiphanies, or theophanies people had, they were too filtered, too contextualized, too biased to be able to definitely state, "This is what God is like." Yes, there were visions and revelations, there were epiphanies and theophanies, but they were not the final word on God. They were part of a journey of discovery that would ultimately lead to the final word on God—Jesus Christ. John will contradict whatever he is forced to contradict—even the Old Testament if necessary—in order to insist on saying, "No one has ever seen God." But John only says this so that he can say what he really wants to say—"It is God the only Son, who is close to the Father's heart, who has made him known."* John insists on saying no one has ever seen God so that he can say, "But now we have seen God!" When we see Jesus, we see God! In Christ we see God—not in a filtered theophany—but in the form of human flesh! Jesus is the final word on God. God is like Jesus. God has always been like Jesus. There has never been a time when God was not like Jesus. We have not always known this, but now we do.

God is like Jesus, and Jesus is like the Beatitudes. To the extent we don't understand the Beatitudes—and they are deeply counterintuitive—to the same extent we don't understand the nature of God. The Mercy Beatitude captures the tone and tenor of Jesus's personality. Jesus consistently exhibited mercy and commended mercy. The only people toward whom Jesus was not merciful were the unmerciful. This is why spiritual pride and withholding mercy are the most dangerous sins a person can commit. With the mercy of God there is always hope, even for the worst of sinners. But if we think we need no mercy and extend no mercy to others, we cut ourselves off from the mercy of God. It is only those who are alienated from the mercy of God who are truly lost.

If we hold the fourth and fifth beatitudes together—the Justice and Mercy Beatitudes—we get a deliberate echo of

---

* John 1:18

Micah 6:8, where we are told to "do justice" and "love mercy." The Mercy Beatitude doesn't stand by itself—it stands in tension with the Justice Beatitude. Without a commitment to justice, mercy can collapse into a cheap sentimentality that is nothing more than the saccharine advice to "be nice." But the passion for justice must be tempered by a deep commitment to mercy, or we end up justifying viciousness in the name of justice. Justice without mercy is cruel, and it is not like God. We live in the tension of longing for justice but always extending mercy. This cruel world needs more mercy, and where is this cruel world to find more mercy if not from the followers of Jesus?

Living in the tension of justice and mercy can at times place us in difficult ethical dilemmas. When should we press for justice, and when should we plead for mercy? It may not always be easy to know, but when in doubt, go with mercy. Mercy should be our default mode. The apostle James said it like this: "Judgment will be without mercy to anyone who has shown no mercy; mercy triumphs over judgment."* "Mercy triumphs over judgment" would be a good motto for those wanting to model the beauty of Christ in the ugly world of cold, hard justice. If our churches are to be anything like a shelter from the storm, we must become famous for our mercy. But is this our reputation? If people find themselves in need of mercy, is their first thought to find an evangelical church? If not, then we need to change. Why were sinners attracted to Jesus and evidently felt quite comfortable around him? The answer is simple. In Jesus they found mercy. If people really believe they

---

* James 2:13

can find mercy in our churches, they will come to us like way-farers caught in a storm in search of safe haven.

---

Blessed are the pure in heart, for they will see God.
—MATTHEW 5:8

*Blessed are those who have a clean window into their*
    *soul,*
*For they will perceive God when and where others don't.*

The specific blessing that Jesus promises to the pure in heart in the sixth beatitude is that they will see God. Again, we are reminded that the apostle John said no one has ever seen God, but that to see Christ is to at last see God. Yet as we consider the ministry of Jesus as recorded in the Gospels, it is evident that some recognized God at work in the life and ministry of Christ, while others did not. It is one of the ironies of the Gospels that the sinful and irreligious were often quicker to recognize Jesus as a man sent by God than the devout and religious. At the crucifixion, the chief priests mocked Jesus's claim to be the Son of God, while the pagan centurion reverently confessed Jesus as the Son of God.* Most notably it was the religious and conservative Pharisees who failed to recognize that the work of God was being accomplished through Jesus of Nazareth. Consequently Jesus repeatedly described the Pharisees as blind, calling them, "blind Pharisees,"†

---

\* See Matthew 27:39–43, 54.

† Matthew 23:26

"blind men,"* "blind guides,"† and "blind fools."‡ How are we to understand this? What was the reason for their spiritual blindness? According to the sixth beatitude, the ability to see God has to do with the purity of our heart.

The word used for "purity" as a description of the heart is simply the word *clean*. Jesus says it is those who possess a clean heart who can see God. There is a sense in which the heart or soul is an organ of perception. The apostle Paul speaks of the eyes of the heart, and Jesus talks about eyes as the window of the soul.§ The heart of man is like a window, which, if clean, can perceive God at work in the world. Conversely, if the window of the human heart is covered with a darkening grime, the result is a kind of spiritual blindness.

But the cleanness of heart that enables us to see God may ✕ not be what you think it is. It's not the morally upright or ethically irreproachable who have clean hearts (as commendable as these things may be); rather, cleanness of heart has to do with a lack of pride, hypocrisy, and judgmentalism. Overconfidence in our ability to see, producing the deception that we can accurately judge others, is in reality a form of spiritual blindness. As it says in the Talmud, "We do not see things as they are; we see things as we are." This is made abundantly clear in one of Jesus's more contentious dialogues with the Pharisees after he had healed a man who was born blind.

> Jesus said, "I came into this world for judgment so that those who do not see may see, and those who do see may become blind." Some of the Pharisees near

---

\* Matthew 23:19, esv
† Matthew 15:14; 23:16
‡ Matthew 23:17
§ Ephesians 1:18; Matthew 6:22–23

him heard this and said to him, "Surely we are not blind, are we?" Jesus said to them, "If you were blind, you would not have sin. But now that you say, 'We see,' your sin remains."

—JOHN 9:39–41

What Jesus says here is full of irony. It was the Pharisees' claim that they could see that kept them blind. When dealing with Jesus, it is the blind who end up seeing and the seeing who end up blind. Because the Pharisees thought they could see everything clearly, and thus were qualified to judge others, they remained completely blind. If they had been honest with themselves and in humility acknowledged that because of their own sin and their own human limitations they had a propensity to misjudge and misinterpret and therefore did not trust their own ability to judge others, then they could have recognized the work of God in Christ and could have begun the process of learning how to see in the light of Christ. But instead, their own spiritual pride condemned them to their own spiritual darkness. The same window that allows light in so that we can see our own sin is also the window by which we can look outward and see God at work in the world. Those who claim to be qualified to judge others because of their own supposed moral superiority are, in fact, living in profound spiritual darkness. The window of their soul is so covered over with the grime of hypocrisy and spiritual pride that it neither allows light in nor allows them to see out. It is only as we confess that we don't see well enough to judge others that we begin to see. And what we begin to see is not sin but God. This is the blessing of the sixth beatitude.

We see the eternal and invisible God only in incarnation. Apart from incarnation, "no one has ever seen God." Of course the supreme incarnation of God is the Incarnation of Christ. But God continues his work in the world through incarnation in the lives of ordinary people who are willing to love and serve others in the name of Christ. If we are corrupted by pride and possess a judgmental disposition, we will never be able to see God at work in the lives of flawed human beings. We will only see their sin and never see God. I think this phenomenon alone explains why Christopher Hitchens could write a ninety-eight-page polemic against Mother Teresa![8] Portraying Mother Teresa as a fraud with dubious motives is not the result of keen insight but the consequences of a tragic blindness. If because of a darkened disposition we only want to see the sins and flaws of others—that's all we will ever see. People afflicted with this malady will often flatter themselves as highly perceptive for their ability to see the peccadilloes of others, but in reality they are simply blind.

If in humility we acknowledge our own sins and flaws, disqualifying ourselves to judge others, that is when we at last begin to see! And what we will see will surprise us. Instead of seeing the sins and shortcomings of others, we will see God unexpectedly at work in the lives of ordinary people, even sinners. Sometimes the world becomes a much more beautiful place simply by being able to see God—to see God present in the lives of others. In this case it's true—beauty lies in the eye of the beholder.

---

Blessed are the peacemakers, for they will be called children of God.

—MATTHEW 5:9

> *Blessed are the peaceful bridge builders in a war-torn*
>   *world,*
> *For they are God's children working in the family*
>   *business.*

To understand the seventh beatitude, we must first liberate the concept of peace from the shrunken way we tend to limit it in Christian vernacular. Yes, Jesus brings inner peace, emotional peace, spiritual peace, peace of mind. But that's not all. The peace of Christ transcends the realm of personal emotions. In a world drunk on hate and tearing itself apart in hostility, the reign of Christ brings peace in the fullest sense of the word. This is how the prophets envisioned Messiah as they spoke of him as the Prince of Peace whose government brings everlasting peace.* To deny Christ the title of Prince of Peace *here and now* is to deny the full reign of Christ.

When Jesus was born, the ruler of the world was Caesar Augustus, and among his imperial titles borne on Roman coins were the designations "Prince of Peace" and "Bringer of World Peace." And in a sense it was true. The Roman Empire did bring a kind of peace, but it was a peace founded on violence and the brutal quashing of all dissent. It was the peace achieved by the Roman cross as an instrument of violence. Jesus would bring the world a new kind of peace through a radical reenvisioning of the same Roman cross. Less than twelve hours before his crucifixion, Jesus said, "Peace I leave with you; my peace I give to you. I do not give to you as the world gives."† Perhaps we can understand Jesus as saying something like this: "In my death I am leaving you a new way to peace. I am giving you my peace, but not in the way the world gives

---

* Isaiah 9:6–7
† John 14:27

peace." How did the Roman world give peace? Through violence. The *Pax Romana* was achieved by identifying others as enemies and fighting against them until they could no longer fight back. And how did Christ give the world peace? By forgiveness. The *Pax Christus* achieves peace by forgiving enemies and embracing them as friends. The peace the world attempts to give (without lasting success) is through violence; Christ gives peace through forgiveness. As disciples of Christ, we are called to embrace forgiveness as the radical alternative to violence. Ultimately we cannot eliminate enemies through violence—violence only multiplies enemies. The only way to eliminate enemies is to love them, forgive them, and seek to reconcile with them as friends. Impractical? Perhaps. But only if you are willing to dismiss Christ as impractical.

The followers of Jesus are called to be peacemakers by modeling the renunciation of violence in favor of forgiveness. This  is exactly what Jesus did with the cross—he took the ultimate instrument of violence and turned it into the ultimate emblem of forgiveness. It is not the peace of force and violence that Jesus gives the world—Caesar had already given that. Rather it is the peace of love and forgiveness that Jesus gives the world. When Jesus blesses the peacemakers—those who seek to bring peace in places of hostility—he is blessing those who make peace the way *he* makes peace. So we have to constantly ask ourselves, whose way of peacemaking do we really believe in—the Roman way or the Christian way? The way of Caesar or the way of Christ? As long as we feel we can justify violence as a legitimate way to bring about peace, we will eventually resort to it. To take up the cross and follow Jesus is to renounce violence in favor of forgiveness.

As Christians we will do the world a great service and

lead the way in peacemaking if we will boldly and unequivocally state that violence can never be justified in the name of God. Never. If the state feels that violence is unavoidable in achieving their ends, so be it, but the church must speak with a unified voice and tell the state they employ violence without the blessing of God. The church must never again endorse storm troopers wearing belt buckles claiming, *Gott Mit Uns* (God With Us). The bankrupt idea that peace can be achieved by violence was once and for all shamed by the Son of God when he died on a Roman cross renouncing force in favor of forgiveness as the ultimate expression of God's universal love.

In attempting to be a Christian peacemaker, I have forged a friendship with a Jewish artist born in Israel and a Muslim scientist born in Egypt. In various ways we have attempted to demonstrate, that despite our religious differences, we have found a way to work together for peace and the common good. Together we have collected thousands of toys to be distributed to poor Israeli and Palestinian children in and around Gaza. In an effort to explain our cooperation, I drafted this statement on behalf of the three of us.

## FOR THE COMMON GOOD

We are Jews, Christians, and Muslims.
And we are friends.
We seek to follow our respective religions faithfully.
We do not believe all religions are the same.
We recognize the reality of our religious differences.
But we are friends.
We are devout in our faith and respectful of our
    friendship.
Our faith and friendship need not be mutually
    exclusive.

We recognize that we share common space—
The common space of a shared planet.
For the sake of the common good we seek common
 ground.
We do not share a common faith, but we share a
 common humanity.
In our different religions we do not practice the same
 rituals or pray the same prayers.
But in our shared humanity we hold to a common
 dream: Shalom, Salaam, Peace.
We hold to the dream that our children may play in
 peace without fear of violence.
And so...
We pledge not to hate.
We pledge not to dehumanize others.
We pledge to do no harm in the name of God.
As individuals we do not compromise the truth
 claims of our respective religions.
But we will not use truth claims to fuel hate or
 justify violence.
We will practice our respective faiths: Judaism,
 Christianity, Islam.
But we believe our faith can be practiced in the way
 of peace—
We believe our faith truly practiced need never be at
 odds with humanitarian ideals.
Our religions share a complex and intertwined
 history—
A history of interaction that has too often been
 tumultuous and bloody.
We believe there must be a better way, and we seek
 that better way.
The way of peace.
We are Jews, Christians, and Muslims.
And we are friends.

We seek common ground for the common good.
Shalom, Salaam, Peace.

—AHMED EL-SHERIF
—SAMUEL NACHUM
—BRIAN ZAHND

Some have asked if my statement implies a concession not to proselytize for the sake of peaceful coexistence. No. My statement does not preclude evangelizing Muslims or Jews; it precludes endorsing hatred and violence in the name of Christ. I confess Jesus is Lord. I believe in proclaiming the gospel. I am for sharing the gospel of Jesus Christ with everyone, including Muslims and Jews. But Christianity and Judaism have been coexisting for two thousand years, and Christianity and Islam have been coexisting fourteen centuries. Unfortunately these relations have not always been peaceful. Today there are 1.3 billion Muslims, and in a world that has suffered deeply from religiously inspired violence, we must find a way to live together in peace. Furthermore, peaceful dialogue is far more conducive to fruitful evangelism than entrenched hostility. So while seeking to proclaim the gospel of Jesus Christ to my Jewish and Muslim neighbors, I am more than willing to pledge to do them no harm and to respect their humanity. I am quite certain Jesus is not opposed to this!

When I invited my Jewish and Muslim friends to join me on a Sunday morning for a "kitchen table conversation" about how Jews, Christians, and Muslims can live together in peace, it was one of the most memorable Sundays in the history of our church. I specifically spoke to Samuel Nachum and Ahmed El-Sherif about how Jesus had said, "Blessed are the peacemakers, for they will be called children of God." Neither of them knew Jesus had said this. I found that both amazing and sad. When Ahmed was first invited to join me for a Sunday morning service, he initially expressed hesitation. Having identified our church as an evangelical congregation, he said, "Those are the kind of people who hate me." How sad, how tragic, that a Muslim would identify evangelical Christians as those who hate Muslims. But on that Sunday as the three of us talked together about how we must love one another and learn to live together in peace, and as I explained how the pogroms and crusades did not represent the love of Christ, the tears flowed freely throughout the auditorium, and nearly everyone described what had happened with the same word—beautiful.

---

Blessed are those who are persecuted for righteousness' sake, for theirs is the kingdom of heaven.

—MATTHEW 5:10

*Blessed are those who are mocked and misunderstood for
    the right reasons,
For the kingdom of heaven comes to earth amidst much
    persecution.*

With the eighth and final beatitude, the blessings that Jesus bestows upon those who welcome the kingdom of God come full circle. Jesus began by blessing the poor in spirit with the kingdom of heaven, and in the final beatitude Jesus bestows the same blessing upon those who are persecuted for righteousness' sake. Why the repetition of a blessing? Jesus isn't "recycling" a blessing because he ran out of ideas. Jesus understands that those who welcome the reign of righteousness that comes from the kingdom of heaven will often find themselves at odds with the principalities and powers who run the current regimes. Jesus blessed those who are persecuted for the right reason with the kingdom of heaven, because the kingdom of heaven only comes to earth amidst much persecution. It is also significant that this beatitude follows the Peacemakers Beatitude. In a world built around an axis of power enforced by violence, to be a prophetic voice for the way of peace often leads to persecution—persecution that can run the gamut from mild ridicule to deadly violence. This is seen most clearly in Jesus's own life. The Beatitudes lead us into the life of the kingdom of God. They also lead us into the way of the cross. The hill of the Beatitudes and the hill of Calvary are not unrelated. The moment Jesus proclaimed the Beatitudes on that Galilean hillside—and began to live them—he was launched on a course that would ultimately lead to Good Friday and his crucifixion on the hill of Calvary.

---

The beauty that saves the world is the beauty of the cruciform. In a kind of majestic passion play we find the beauty of the Beatitudes on full display at Calvary. The cross is nothing less than Jesus giving the last full measure of devotion to the saving beauty found in the Beatitudes. As Jesus dies upon the cross, forgiving his enemies, while priests mock, women weep, a thief repents, and a soldier makes a creedal confession, all eight blessings of the Beatitudes are played out in dramatic form.

*Blessed are the poor in spirit, for theirs is the kingdom of heaven.* Who is promised heaven at Calvary? Not the spiritually rich

Pharisees, but the spiritually bankrupt thief who is crucified next to Christ.

*Blessed are those who mourn, for they will be comforted.* Who are the mourners at Calvary? The faithful women who had followed Jesus from Galilee. And who are the first to receive the comfort of Easter Sunday? Those very same women!

*Blessed are the meek, for they will inherit the earth.* Jesus had entered Jerusalem five days earlier, meek, riding on a donkey. For making the improbable claim to being a king, Jesus was crucified. But who has received the nations as his inheritance, and whose kingdom now reaches from sea to sea? The Lord Jesus Christ!

*Blessed are those who hunger and thirst for righteousness, for they will be filled.* What is Jesus doing as he hangs upon the cross and cries out, "I am thirsty"?* He is setting the world right. He is giving the world a new axis. As Maltbie Babcock said in his famous hymn, "Jesus who died shall be satisfied, and earth and heaven be one."[9]

*Blessed are the merciful, for they will receive mercy.* It was the thief who expressed mercy to Jesus as he was being mocked who receives mercy and the promise of paradise.

*Blessed are the pure in heart, for they will see God.* It was the pagan soldier who made no claims of spiritual insight who was able to see in Jesus what the chief priests could not see.

*Blessed are the peacemakers, for they will be called children of God.* Jesus had refused to take up the sword or call upon armies of avenging angels and perpetuate the cycle of violence. Instead he made peace by the blood of the cross. And in his

---

* John 19:28

death the Roman centurion made the beatific pronouncement, "Truly this was the Son of God!"*

*Blessed are those who are persecuted for righteousness' sake, for theirs is the kingdom of heaven.* Jesus was persecuted for righteousness' sake by the principalities and powers, but it is at the cross that God begins to remake the world according to righteousness, and it is at the cross that the reign of the kingdom of heaven begins. Truly Christ upon the cross is Jesus living his own Beatitudes.

---

X The cruciform is the beauty that saves the world. The cruciform is the beauty of the Beatitudes in full flower. The Beatitudes and the cruciform are ultimately the same thing—one existing in proclamation, the other existing in demonstration. It is this beauty that we are called to emulate as followers of Jesus Christ. The ethos of the Beatitudes and the pathos of the cruciform must be that which gives us our distinctive beauty. Churches shaped by the Beatitudes and formed by the cruciform will be a shelter from the storm to the beleaguered masses of humanity who long for something other than the ugly and unforgiving pragmatism offered by the principalities and powers. Yes, this is the beauty we must embrace! The beauty of co-suffering love as defined by the Beatitudes and demonstrated by the cross. For far too long we have kept the Beatitudes and Calvary artificially separated. By thinking of the cross in a mechanistic manner and evaluating it as a kind of economic transaction, we have falsely imagined that what Jesus did on the cross was entirely unrelated to what he was

---

* Matthew 27:54, ESV

preaching when he began his ministry in Galilee. This is a tragic mistake, a mistake that hopefully the church is beginning to realize and recover from. The commencement and culmination of the ministry of Christ are inseparably connected. The Beatitudes and the cruciform are the same thing. They are God's saving beauty. The beauty of the Beatitudes leads to the beauty of the cruciform, and together they form the beauty that will save the world.

## Book Epigraph

1. C. S. Lewis, *The Weight of Glory* (New York: HarperCollins, 2001), 42.

2. Miguel de Cervantes, *Don Quixote* (New York: HarperCollins, 2003), 327.

## Prelude

1. *Primary Chronicle of the Sent by Prince Vladimir of Kiev-Rus to Constantinople*, as quoted in *The Story of Christianity* by David Bentley Hart, *The Story of Christianity* (n.p.: Quercus Books, 2008), 125.

2. Fyodor Dostoevsky, *The Idiot*, Alan Meyers, trans. (Oxford: Oxford University Press, 2008).

3. Yves M.-J. Congar, "The Reasons for the Unbelief of Our Time: A Theological Conclusion," *Integr* (December 1938), 21, as quoted in Hans Boersma, *Nouvelle Théolgie and Sacramental Ontology* (New York: Oxford University Press, 2009), 1.

4. Vigen Guroian, *The Melody of Faith: Theology in an Orthodox Key* (Grand Rapids, MI: Wm. B. Eerdmans, 2010), 7.

5. Friedrich Nietzsche, *Twilight of the Idols* (New York: Oxford University Press, 2009), 9.

6. Walt Whitman, "Finally Comes the Poet," *Leaves of Grass* (Redford, VA: Wilder Publications, 2007).

## CHAPTER 1
## FORM AND BEAUTY

1. Origen, *Contra Celsum*, 1.30, as referenced in David Bentley Hart, *The Beauty of the Infinite* (Grand Rapids, MI: Wm. B. Eerdmans, 2004), 3.

2. Hart, *The Beauty of the Infinite*, 3.

3. Russell Moore, "God, the Gospel, and Glenn Beck," *Moore to the Point* (blog), August 29, 2010, http://www .russellmoore.com/2010/08/29/god-the-gospel-and-glenn -beck/ (accessed June 27, 2011).

4. Stanley Hauerwas and William H. Willimon, *Resident Aliens* (Nashville, TN: Abingdon Press, 1989), 43.

5. Lazar Puhalo, "Faith, Freedom and the Human Vocation," an invited paper presented at *The Risali-i Nur: Faith, Morality and the Future of Humankind*, an international conference of The Istanbul Foundation for Science and Culture, October 3–5, 2010, http://www.clarion-journal .com/files/faith_freedom_archbishop_lazar.pdf (accessed June 27, 2011).

6. Stanley Hauerwas, *Hannah's Child* (Grand Rapids, MI: Wm. B. Eerdmans, 2010), 274.

7. Hart, *The Beauty of the Infinite*, 122.

8. "Not Dark Yet" by Bob Dylan, copyright © 1997 by Special Rider Music. All rights reserved. International copyright secured. Reprinted by permission.

9. Francis J. Ambrosio, "Meaning—a Question and a Commitment," lecture 1 of *Philosophy, Religion, and the Meaning of Life*, Teaching Company Lecture Series, transcript viewed at http://teachingcompany.12.forumer .com/viewtopic.php?t=2726 (accessed June 28, 2011). Course description available at http://www.thegreatcourses.com

/tgc/courses/Course_Detail.aspx?cid=4610 (accessed June 28, 2011).

10. Hans Urs von Balthasar, *Love Alone Is Credible* (San Francisco, CA: Ignatius Press, 2004), 101–102.

11. Roger Scruton, *Beauty* (New York: Oxford University Press, 2011).

## CHAPTER 2
## THE GREATEST WONDER OF ALL

1. *New Oxford American Dictionary* (New York: Oxford University Press, 2005), s.v. "wonder."

2. Søren Kierkegaard, *Either/Or* (New York: Penguin Classics, 1992), 185.

3. Yuichi Konno, "My Art Is Not an Answer—It Is a Question," interview with Gottfried Helnwein, *Yaso*, September 5, 2003, http://www.helnwein.info/Press_and_Media/495/my_art_is_not_an_answer-it_is_a_question.html (accessed June 28, 2011).

4. Ravi Zacharias, *Recapture the Wonder* (Nashville, TN: Thomas Nelson, 2005), 6.

5. Ann H. Zwinger and Beatrice E. Willard, *Land Above the Trees: A Guide to American Alpine Tundra* (Boulder, CO: Johnson Books, 1996), 3.

6. Hans Urs von Balthasar, *Prayer* (San Francisco, CA: Ignatius Press, 1986), 172.

7. Vladimir Lossky, *In the Image and Likeness of God* (Yonkers, NY: St. Vladimirs Seminary Press, 2001), 202.

8. Aidan Nichols, *Redeeming Beauty* (London, UK: Ashgate Publishing Company, 2007), 78.

9.  As quoted in Boersma, *Nouvelle Théolgie and Sacramental Ontology*.

10. Blaise Pascal, *Pensées* (Oxford, UK: Benediction Classics, 2011), 45.

11. C. S. Lewis, *The Screwtape Letters* (New York: HarperCollins, 2001), 39.

12. Fyodor Dostoevsky, *The Brothers Karamazov* (New York: Bantam Classics, 1984).

13. Søren Kierkegaard, *Journals and Papers* (Bloomington, IN: Indiana University Press, 1967).

14. Aldous Huxley, *Brave New World Revisited* (New York: Harper Perennial Modern Classics, 2006), 120–121.

15. Juvenal, *Sixteen Satires* (New York: Penguin Classics, 1999).

16. John Howard Yoder, *The War of the Lamb* (Grand Rapids, MI: Brazos Press, 2009), 40.

17. *The Fellowship of the Ring*, directed by Peter Jackson (2001; Los Angeles: New Line Home Entertainment, 2002), DVD.

## CHAPTER 3
## AXIS OF LOVE

1.  Wendell Berry, *Hannah Coulter* (Berkeley, CA: Shoemaker & Hoard, 2005), 168.

2.  "Things Have Changed" by Bob Dylan, copyright © 1999 by Special Rider Music. All rights reserved. International copyright secured. Reprinted by permission.

3.  "The Apostles' Creed," Modern English Version, http://www.creeds.net/ancient/apostles.htm (accessed June 29, 2011).

4.  Von Balthasar, *Love Alone Is Credible*.

5. Thomas Hobbes, *Leviathan* (New York: Oxford University Press, 2009), 66, 84.

6. Lord Acton, *Essays on Freedom and Power* (Auburn, AL: Ludwig von Mises Institute, 2010), xi.

7. Wendell Berry, "Some Further Words," *Given: Poems* (Berkeley, CA: Counterpoint, 2006), 28.

8. Stanley Hauerwas, *Cross-Shattered Christ* (Grand Rapids, MI: Brazos Press, 2011).

9. Tertullian, *Apologeticus* 50, translated by S. Thelwall, Christian Classics Ethereal Library, http://www.tertullian .org/anf/anf03/anf03-05.htm#P478_246152 (accessed June 29, 2011).

10. Hart, *The Beauty of the Infinite*, 441.

11. Robyn Keeler and David J. Pennoyer, "More on the Murder of Pastor Dritan Prroj," IPHC.org, October 15, 2010, http:// www.iphc.org/news/more-murder-pastor-dritan-prroj (accessed June 29, 2011).

12. Taken from an e-mail to author from Erik Stensland, October 23, 2010.

## CHAPTER 4
## EAST OF EDEN

1. John Steinbeck, *East of Eden* (New York: Penguin, 1952, 2002), 264.

2. Hart, *The Beauty of the Infinite*, 33.

3. Bruno Forte, *The Portal of Beauty* (Grand Rapids, MI: Wm. B. Eerdmans , 2008), 51–52.

4. Friedrich Nietzsche, *Beyond Good and Evil* (Lindenhurst, NY: Tribeca Books, 2011).

5.  *The Fellowship of the Ring*, directed by Peter Jackson (2001; Los Angeles: New Line Home Entertainment, 2002), DVD.

6.  Yoder, *The War of the Lamb*, 8.

7.  Father Christian de Chergé, as quoted in Hauerwas, *Cross-Shattered Christ*.

8.  Hauerwas, *Cross-Shattered Christ*.

9.  N. T. Wright, "Revelation and Christian Hope: Political Implications of the Revelation to John," a lecture given at Duke Divinity School, October 26, 2010.

10. "Marching to Zion" by Isaac Watts. Public domain.

## CHAPTER 5
## I AM FROM THE FUTURE

1.  From the poem "Manifesto: The Mad Farmer Liberation Front," *The Selected Poems of Wendell Berry* (Berkeley, CA: Counterpoint, 1999).

2.  Frederick Douglass, *Narrative of the Life of Frederick Douglass: An American Slave, Written by Himself* (New York: Modern Library, an imprint of the Random House Publishing Group, 2004), 64.

3.  From the PBS film *God in America: "A Nation Reborn,"* directed by Sarah Colt, transcript viewed at http://www.pbs.org/godinamerica/transcripts/hour-three.html (accessed July 7, 2011).

4.  Douglass, *Narrative of the Life of Frederick Douglass: An American Slave, Written by Himself*, 113, 115.

5.  Lillian Smith, "Introduction to the 1994 Edition," in *Killers of the Dream*, (New York: W. W. Norton & Company, 1994), 8.

6.  Smith, *Killers of the Dream*, 27, 29.

7. Eugene Peterson, *Practice Resurrection* (Grand Rapids, MI: Wm. B. Eerdmans, 2010), 13.

8. Yoder, *The War of the Lamb*, 54.

## CHAPTER 6
## A CATHEDRAL OF ASTONISHMENT

1. As quoted in Rosette C. Lamont, *Ionesco: A Collection of Critical Essays* (Englewood Cliffs, NJ: Prentice-Hall, 1973), 167.

2. As quoted in Abe Arkoff, *Psychology and Personal Growth*, 4th ed. (n.p.: Allyn and Bacon, 1993), 300.

3. Hans Urs von Balthasar, *Theo-Logic: Truth of the World* (San Francisco, CA: Ignatius Press, 2000), 209.

4. E-mail to author from Devree Chleborad, December 1, 2010.

5. Oscar Wilde, *The Picture of Dorian Gray* (Lindenhurst, NY: Tribeca Books, 2011), preface.

6. Salman Rushdie, *Step Across This Line* (New York: Random House, 2002), 171–172.

7. Eugene Peterson, *Christ Plays in Ten Thousand Places* (Grand Rapids, MI: Wm. B. Eerdmans, 2009), 147.

## CHAPTER 7
## A SHELTER FROM THE STORM

1. "Shelter From the Storm" by Bob Dylan, copyright © 1974, renewed 2002 by Ram's Horn Music. All rights reserved. International copyright secured. Reprinted by permission.

2. Anup Shah, "Poverty Facts and Stats," GlobalIssues.org, September 20, 2010, http://www.globalissues.org/article/26 /poverty-facts-and-stats#src1 (accessed July 11, 2011).

3. Ibid.

4. Ibid.

5. CNN.com, "UN Chief: Hunger Kills 17,000 Kids Daily," November 17, 2009, http://www.cnn.com/2009/WORLD /europe/11/17/italy.food.summit/index.html (accessed July 12, 2011).

6. Anup Shah, "World Military Spending," GlobalIssues.org, May 2, 2011, http://www.globalissues.org/article/75/world -military-spending#WorldMilitarySpending (accessed July 12, 2011).

7. Jacob Neusner, *A Rabbi Talks With Jesus* (Montreal, Quebec: McGill-Queen's University Press, 2000), 68.

8. Christopher Hitchens, *The Missionary Position: Mother Teresa in Theory and Practice* (Brooklyn, NY: Verso, 1997).

9. "This Is My Father's World" by Maltbie Babcock. Public domain.

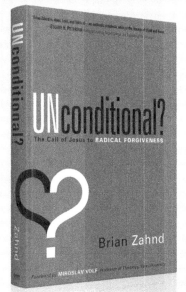

# WHAT DO YOU DO WHEN TROUBLE COMES?

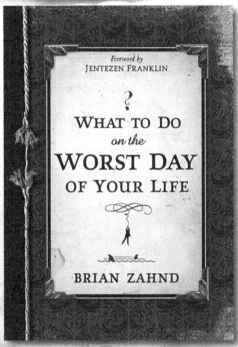

978-1-59979-726-7 / $14.99

"My wife and I have read and reread every word in this book. It was like God's voice to us in one of the toughest seasons of our lives."
—Jentezen Franklin, *New York Times* best-selling author of *Fasting*

The life of King David gives us a timeless model for how to experience God's restorative power in the midst of deep tragedy. Discover the steps you can take to recover from all life's challenges.